B R A I N
STORMS

To Rachel, a person
I am glad to call
my friend. Best
wishes and God bless.

Leo Duncan

B R A I N
STORMS

SURVIVING • CATASTROPHIC • ILLNESS

LES DUNCAN

TATE PUBLISHING & *Enterprises*

Published by Tate Publishing & Enterprises, LLC
127 E. Trade Center Terrace | Mustang, Oklahoma 73064 USA
1.888.361.9473 | www.tatepublishing.com

Tate Publishing is committed to excellence in the publishing industry. The company reflects the philosophy established by the founders, based on Psalm 68:11,
"The Lord gave the word and great was the company of those who published it."

Book design copyright © 2007 by Tate Publishing, LLC. All rights reserved.
Cover design by Janae J. Glass
Interior design by Elizabeth A. Mason

Published in the United States of America

ISBN: 978-1-60462-223-2
1. Self-Help: Motivational & Inspirational
2. Medical: Neurology: General
07.11.29

To my sons–Dave, Doug, & Mike
Thank you for the joy and happiness you bring to my life

To my many doctors, nurses, therapists, and caregivers
Especially my neurosurgeons
Dr. Jonathan White–Dallas, TX
Dr. Yoshiro Takaoka–Cleveland, OH
May God bless you for the work you do.

And to my wife, Sharon
She's the best!

TABLE OF CONTENTS

Foreword 9

Introduction 15

Humor Therapy 21

Mind, Body and Spirit 27

The Process 31

Listen to Your Body 43

The Word 51

Hire an Exceptional Doctor 57

Get Your Personal Affairs in Order 67

Set Up a Communication Chain 73

So, How Are You Doing? 79

Be a Nuisance 85

Avoid the Blame Game 95

No Stinkin' Thinkin' 99

Make Recovery Your Full Time Job 105

Pace Yourself 113

Setbacks 121

The Virtue of Patience 127

It's Only Temporary 133

The Good, the Bad, and the Ugly 137

Be an Inspiration to Others 145

Do I Have Cooties? 149

Bad Things do Happen to Good People 155

There Is No Place Like Home 159

The Power of Prayer 163

Look for the Greater Good   173
Stay in the Present Moment   179
Be Kind—Especially to Your Caregivers   187
The New Normal   193
Conclusion   197
Afterword   201
Endnotes   203

FOREWORD

I grew up in the small Midwest City of Wichita, Kansas. About 260,000 people lived there when I was a young boy. The local newspaper ran a column titled "Usual and Unusual" which featured interesting articles about the citizens of Wichita. The journalists who wrote this column mainly hung out in the emergency room of the local hospital, waiting for something out of the ordinary to report on.

Between the age of three and nineteen, I was the feature item in this column nine times—in the "unusual" category. The headlines read as follows:

TWO-YEAR OLD BOY FALLS DOWN
BASEMENT STEPS.
KNOCKS OUT ALL HIS BABY TEETH

Actually I didn't knock all of them out–many of them just broke off. They cut and pulled the broken ones out of my gums in the emergency room. Ouch!

FIVE-YEAR OLD BOY CUTS HEAD WHILE CRAWLING UNDER HIS KINDERGARTEN EASEL—REQUIRES 12 STITCHES

I was just trying to get to my cubbyhole. Boy there was a lot of blood!

FIVE-YEAR OLD BOY BREAKS COLLARBONE AFTER FALLING OUT OF TOP BUNK BED

It happened in the middle of the night. I just got up and went back to bed. I didn't notice the pain until the next morning. And if this wasn't enough...

FIVE-YEAR OLD BOY RE-BREAKS COLLARBONE IN SAND PILE INCIDENT

I was at recess, with my broken collarbone immobilized with bandages and a sling, when I thought it would be fun to let the other kids bury me in the sand pile. Afterward, I realized I had a lot of sand inside the wrappings, so I took them off to get clean. Snap, the collarbone broke again.

TEN-YEAR OLD BOY RUNS OVER HIMSELF WITH SLED

I was going down a snow packed hill on my wooden red flyer sled with metal runners. I was about to collide with another boy on the sled just in front of me, so I instinctively reached my hand and arm out in front of me to slow myself down. Instead, I ran over my wrist.

Twelve-year old boy steps on 16-penny rusty nail. Penetrates entire foot

I was *running* in a field when I stepped squarely onto a rusty 16-penny nail housed in a once inch by four inch piece of lumber. The nail had passed all the way through my foot and the sharp end was protruding out the top. I limped into the house where my uncle grabbed hold of the wooden board housing the nail, and pulled it swiftly out of my foot. Boy that hurt!

Thirteen-year old boy bites his tongue—requires four stitches to stop bleeding

Stitches in the tongue—double ouch!

Eighteen-year old man burns skin in factory's acid tank

I was working my way through school in a factory, nickel-plating some metal and got carried away.

Nineteen-year old college student victim of drive by shooting

I was working in an oil refinery earning money to pay my college tuition when a large white car came cruising down a nearby road. The next thing I knew, a gun barrel was sticking out of the back car window and I was dodging bullets.

I didn't know these guys and they didn't know me. It was during the 1969 race riots and I just happened to be in the wrong place at the wrong time.

If I still lived in Wichita and if the local newspaper still ran their "Usual and Unusual" column, I may have just seized another headline.

FIFTY-SEVEN YEAR OLD MAN SURVIVES FOURTH BRAIN HEMORRHAGE AND SECOND BRAIN SURGERY

As I sit in my study at home, I realize it has been just two months since I underwent risky surgery to remove a mass of bleeding blood vessels in my brain. And a little more than three months since I spent Christmas Day in the Intensive Care Unit at the hospital. I reflect on the fact that this was a scary process—for me, for my family, for my coworkers, and for my friends.

Two months ago, I was released from the hospital unable to get around without a walker—I could barely get around with that. Just two months ago, I couldn't stand up without getting dizzy; I had to grab onto things in order not to fall. Two months ago I was unable to dress myself. Two months ago I couldn't see out of my left eye and couldn't hear out of my left ear. Two months ago I couldn't watch TV, read a book, or go to work. Two months ago, I didn't have the strength or the ability to begin writing this book. I could go on and on, but suffice it to say—two months ago I had a long way to go.

What was wrong with me? Technically speaking, I have a genetic condition called cavernous angioma. It is the same condition that caused the death of track star Florence Griffith-Joyner. It is a cousin to the illness suffered by Senator Tim Johnson, D-South Dakota. Doctors also sometimes refer to these as cavernomas, cavernous malformations, cavernous hemangiomas, derbrovascular malformations, and intracranial vascular malformations.

But, enough of the technical terms. What this means in plain English is that I have some messed up blood vessels in my brain. They are the result of several defective genes that have been passed down through my mother's side of the family. They are dark red to blue in color, and look a little bit like small mulberries. Sometimes they rupture and bleed.

Bleeding in the brain is not a good thing. It can cause temporary or permanent nerve damage—resulting in things such as an inability to walk, talk, swallow, see, hear, smell, feel, etc. It can cause the body to go into seizure. It can even cause death.

I am not alone. The condition I have is the most common form of brain vascular malformation in the world. Literally millions of people have it. Most live their entire lives and don't know because, technically, there is only a two-percent chance that a cavernous angioma will bleed.

Like most people who have one of these mulberry-looking malformed veins in their brain, I don't just have one—I have many of them.

Unlike most people, I am a bleeder. I am fifty-seven years old. Two of my cavernous angiomas have bled. In total, I have had four brain hemorrhages and two brain surgeries over the past sixteen years. A total of six tumultuous brain's storms.

I have successfully survived and recovered from all my

previous bleeds and surgeries and I am confident that I will recover from this one as well.

As I begin writing, I am still working hard to recover. I have a long way to go but I know it is possible, because I have recovered before.

Friends and relatives who have seen me at my neurological worst call my recoveries miraculous. Some refer to me as a walking miracle. Still others know that I am a strong, determined, deeply religious man and are not surprised that I have recovered time and time again.

How have I done it? That's what this book is all about. I am not a surgeon, a doctor, a counselor, or a clergyman or clergywoman. I'm an ordinary person, who has firsthand experience dealing with catastrophic illnesses—I've been there and done that not once, not twice, but six times.

I plan to write most of this book while recovering from my last surgery and hemorrhage. So I will be writing it literally as I go through the process of coping with and recovering from a catastrophic illness. My hope is that it will provide hope, inspiration, and sage advice to others facing catastrophic illness. Perhaps that is you or perhaps it is someone you love. God bless you!

INTRODUCTION

It was Wednesday, September 11, 2002—exactly one year after the horrific Al Qaeda's terrorist attacks on our country. I woke up excited that most television and radio networks were devoting virtually their entire programming to tributes of people who were involved in this tragic event. I had my TiVo programmed to tape many of the shows while I was at work, which my wife, Sharon, and I planned to watch over the next few evenings at home.

I rose early—as I usually do. But on that day, I didn't feel well. I had a headache that had been getting progressively worse for several days and I felt a bit spacey. I told myself that I had just been working too hard. It had been a busy year and I really needed a vacation.

A friend of mine had invited me to play golf at an exclusive golf club the next day, and I *needed* to clear my calendar at work before I could do this. Even though I didn't feel all that well, I felt I had to go to work on September 11, 2002, because I really wanted to be off playing golf the next day. In addition, we had a special 9/11 tribute planned at work that I didn't want to miss.

I made my way to the office but I only lasted a few hours. I spent the remainder of the day at home, resting. I went to bed that evening expecting to feel better the next day. I tried not to think the worst. After all, the doctor had told me that the probability of me having *another* brain hemorrhage was low. I had already had two. I figured that should be enough.

I knew the symptoms, and although I was experiencing some of them, they were not nearly as bad as those I had experienced when my brain bled a decade earlier. During the previous episode, I had been unable to stand up. I had crawled back and forth from my bed to the bathroom because I couldn't walk. My wife had to help me dress. I ended up having brain surgery and the doctors removed a faulty blood vessel. It took me nearly twelve months to recover and get back to work. Certainly whatever was happening to me now was not the same thing. *Nothing to worry about*, I told myself. There would be no more surgery performed on my brain.

The next day was Thursday, September 12, 2002. I awoke. I was grateful for that day, just as I had been grateful for each and every day since my first brain hemorrhage. It is true that serious health problems can completely change your attitude toward and your perspective on life.

I was fixing my breakfast, when I suddenly felt much worse. The vision in my left eye was a little blurry. My left ear ached and my hearing was slightly impaired. My head hurt even worse—the pain was almost unbearable. The left side of my face began to feel numb and I had a light tingling sensation in my left leg.

I knew right then that there would be no golf with my friend at a prestigious golf club that day. I think I also knew that I wouldn't be watching tributes to 9/11 with my wife any time soon.

I called to my wife, Sharon, and simply said, "I think

you had better take me to the emergency room—I am having another brain hemorrhage."

At the emergency room they take brain hemorrhages seriously. I was whisked away immediately—ahead of many others who had been waiting to be seen with less serious ailments. They put me in a room and hooked me up to heart, pulse, blood pressure, and other vital sign monitors, and they stuck an oxygen hose in my nostrils. Minutes later I was wheeled away for a CAT Scan. No one said anything, but I could tell from the whispering and grim faces that something was very wrong. I went directly from a CAT Scan to a MRI.

Just minutes later I was back in the emergency room hooked up to all the same monitors and the ER doctor came to tell me what I already knew—my brain was bleeding. He seemed very concerned. He told me that he had called a neurosurgeon, who was expected to arrive any minute.

I looked at my wife and told her that I felt better than I had felt a two hours earlier. I reminded her that my symptoms were still much less severe than with my previous hemorrhage. I knew the drill. The doctor would put me on steroids to reduce the swelling caused by bleeding in the brain, and I would be hospitalized for a few days to make sure the bleeding and swelling stopped and things got better. I would be told to "take it easy" for a few weeks. I was confident this was a minor blip. I remember saying to my wife, "I am a little worried, but I am not panicked."

A few minutes later, the neurosurgeon arrived with the following message:

You have had a serious bleed in the pons area of the brainstem. I want to admit you to the hospital today. I don't know how long you will have to stay. Your activities will be limited until we know for certain that the bleeding has stopped.

The pons area of the brainstem is the worst possible place to have a brain hemorrhage. Frankly, I am surprised that your symptoms aren't more serious. For some reason, you have survived the bleeding and are still in pretty good shape. You are a very lucky man.

But, we will need to remove the source, because the next time this bleeds you may not be so lucky. This will involve very risky brain surgery. Given the location of your bleed, you could become paralyzed, or become unable to speak—and there is a chance you may go into a coma or even die. But if we don't do surgery, the likelihood of these things happening increases.

The problem with the pons area of the brainstem is that every millimeter counts. Doing surgery there is something that neither I nor any other doctor in Texas is qualified to do. This is something that you will want only the finest neurosurgeon to consider.

I plan to refer you to the world's best neurosurgeon in Phoenix, Arizona. He has done many successful operations in this area of the brain. Even then, there is no guarantee that you won't suffer permanent neurological damage from the surgery. This is very serious.

I will check on you again later to make sure you are doing okay.

And then he left—just like that. I turned to my wife and said, "I'm definitely not panicked. I am scared to death."

I consulted with several other neurosurgeons who all recommended against surgery because it was too risky. Even the world's best in Phoenix told me that the surgery was not worth the risk. It is common with these types of bleeds *not* to do surgery on the first bleed, especially when the nerve damage is not severe and the patient is improving on his or her own. I recuperated at home and was back in the office after about three and a half months. It took me about a year to recover completely.

I went about my daily life as normal until Christmas morning 2005. I awoke that morning with the left side of my face drooping—like I had Bell's Palsy. I couldn't close my left eye and the vision in my left eye was double and blurred. I had a pounding headache and was dizzy and wobbly. I felt spacey—like I wasn't completely all there. I couldn't hear out of my left ear.

My son, who was visiting for the holiday, took me to the emergency room where I once again announced that I was having a brain hemorrhage. I spent several days in the intensive care unit (ICU) at Presbyterian Hospital of Dallas and was then transferred to The University of Texas Southwest Hospital, an educational and research facility in Dallas. It turned out there was one neurosurgeon in Dallas—one of the few neurosurgeons in the country—who was qualified to operate on me. This time he recommended surgery. On February 9, 2006, I underwent a very risky brain surgery.

Since then, I have recovered almost remarkably—not because of the surgery. Surgery only removed the possibility of having further bleeds in this area of my brain and kept my nerve damage from getting worse.

I have recovered because, from the day I became sick, I made it my full-time job to get well again. I put all my energy and determination into achieving that goal.

I have recovered because I have had a tremendous support group who have prayed for me, sent me flowers, cards, gifts, and even cooked my meals to keep my spirits up.

I have recovered because I've kept a positive attitude even during the toughest of times.

I have recovered because I took advantage of all the best medical personnel, facilities, and treatments available to me.

But most of all I have recovered through the grace of God.

HUMOR THERAPY

"Humor is by far the most significant activity of the human brain."

Edward De Bono

One thing I've learned through my four brain hemorrhages and two brain surgeries is that it's important to keep a sense of humor. Laughter is the best medicine.

I understand completely that this is easier said than done—been there, done that six times. It's really difficult to keep smiling when you feel horrible. It's really hard to laugh when you feel like crying. It is hard to feel joyful when your body is in pain. It's a challenge to enjoy life when you feel like you've been kicked in the head. I admit that sometimes I had to force a little humor into my sick body, because it was the last thing my mind wanted.

But I quickly learned that humor took my mind off of my troubles. Oftentimes I was in pain and felt as though I'd rather be dead. I felt that my illness was in control of me. In these times, laughter helped. I am convinced that lifting my spirits with laughter hastened my recoveries.

Like everything else I will discuss in this book, I got better at this as my illnesses recurred. After my first brain surgery, I was downtrodden, troubled, and not in good spirits. I withdrew from friends and neighbors, some of whom would have provided some good laugh therapy had I only allowed it.

Now I'm not a doctor and there may be no scientific evidence that laughter can help heal a really sick person, but in my case it seemed to reduce stress—something I really needed. And I'm told that humor does have some positive physical effects on the body such as stimulating the circulatory system, bolstering the immune system, and even lowering blood pressure. I'm also told that cancer patients find that humor provides some pain relief, encourages relaxation, and reduces stress.

Because of the apparent positive affects of laughter on sick people, some hospitals and treatment centers have set up special rooms where humorous materials, and even volunteer comedians, are available to help make sick people laugh. Starting in 1988, Morton Plant Hospital in Clearwater, Florida developed a "comedy cart," loaded with audio cassettes, cartoon albums, video tapes, humorous books, small games and costume parts, props and magic tricks–all designed to make patients chuckle.[1] "A 1999 survey found that about 1 in 5 National Cancer Institute designated treatment centers offered humor therapy as part of their treatment plan."[2]

One of the best sources of humor for me was a friend who had always made me laugh, and continued to do so throughout my illnesses. But I also enjoyed funny videotapes and CD's and Jay Leno—particularly his nightly monologue and his Monday night "Headlines" segment where he reviews unintentional yet whimsical newspaper articles and ads, some of which are due to misspelling and others due to just dumb photography or poor writing. David Letterman and his Top Ten List also made me laugh. And there was nothing like a good Dave Barry book to get me smiling.

My neurosurgeon provided a bit of much-needed humor when he set my surgery date. We were discussing the logistics of the surgery and he told me I would need to come to the hospital the day before for some pre-operation procedures: blood tests, last minute instructions, etc.

Now they are going to tell you that you need to arrive at the hospital at 5:30 a.m. on the day of surgery.

I will tell you what I told my father last year when he was preparing for heart surgery.

We won't start without you.

He went on to tell me that 6:30 a.m. would be good enough.

The many humorous get-well cards I received during my illness were another good source of laughter. I remember one card in particular that really made me laugh aloud.

Now before I reveal the contents of this card I want to make it clear that I have been blessed with great doctors throughout my illnesses. They have done a great job treating my brain hemorrhages and, when required, removing the deformed veins in my brain that look a little bit like small mulberries and sometimes bleed. So I have the utmost respect for my doctors and what they have done for me. I have always received the perfect amount and quality of medical attention. Having said that, one funny card sticks in my mind. It purported to translate things that doctors say into what they really mean.

The Interpreter's Guide to "Doctor speak"

What Your Doctors Says	What Your Doctor Really Means
I'd like to run a few more tests.	I want the sunroof option for my new car.
I'd like you to see a specialist.	I have absolutely no idea what's wrong with you.
Bend over.	Bend over. (Hey some things are bad enough without some deeper meaning.)
Please make a follow-up appointment.	I'd also like the CD player with the five-disk changer.
The nurse will take over from here.	I'm late for my tee time.
I have good news and bad news.	I have bad news.
You'll feel some slight discomfort.	This is going to hurt like heck!
Hmm…that's interesting.	What the heck is *that* thing?
Any history of medical problems in your family?	Can I blame genetics in case I screw up?
This is a highly treatable disease.	How much insurance are you carrying?

After my last surgery, about six weeks into my recovery, I began working on a David Letterman style top ten list of reasons why it wasn't so bad to have brain surgery. At this point I was still homebound (physically unable to leave my home) and really didn't feel like turning on my home computer. But I did it anyway because it was good therapy for me and it would show others following my progress that I was getting "back to normal."

As I mentioned earlier, I love David Letterman and his Top Ten List. Most people who know me know this. I worked on my top ten reasons why it isn't so bad to have brain surgery for about two weeks until I got it the way I wanted it. Then I shared it with those people who had been following my progress. Here is how it came out.

Top ten reasons why it isn't so bad to have brain surgery:

1. Morphine—as much as I want

2. The next time someone calls me "brainless," I have an eyewitness to the contrary—my brain surgeon has seen mine firsthand

3. The waxing I got when they ripped the hospital tape off my arms, chest, and back is worth at least $250 at a good salon

4. I haven't missed a single episode of Oprah

5. I get to taste everyone's favorite recipes (thanks for all the good food!)

6. I've learned that "we'll get that taken care of in a week" in doctor speak means, "you'll be lucky if you ever see me again"

7. My wife gets new carpet because my walking recovery laps repeatedly around the house has worn the old stuff out

8. I don't have to worry about the air pollution index outside because I am stuck inside recuperating

9. Cute nurses—some of them really cute

10. It reinforces the fact that I have the greatest family and friends on earth

There is nothing better for a sick body than laughter. Although it is difficult to smile when you don't feel well, a smile is just the right medicine for healing.

The sicker you are the more you need laughter. Humor stimulates the circulatory system and bolsters the immune system. Humor even lowers blood pressure, reduces pain, and reduces stress. So surround yourself with funny people, funny books, funny tapes—anything that will make you laugh.

And remember: when you get sick, it doesn't just affect you. It affects everyone around you—everyone in your life. By laughing and staying positive, you will help them get through it as well.

MIND, BODY, AND SPIRIT

"A healthy mind is a healthy body."
Junvenal Roman poet & satirist
(55 AD–127 AD)

Another thing I've learned is that recovering from a serious illness is not just about physical health. In fact it's not even *primarily* about physical health.

When I concentrated first and foremost on keeping my spiritual and emotional health in good shape, a return to good physical health was more likely, faster, and more complete.

The fact is that by the time I was diagnosed, I had little control over my physical health—that was in the hands of God and my doctors. But I had immense control over my spiritual and emotional health.

Each time I was clinically diagnosed with a life-threatening condition, I noticed a tendency to feel panic and self-pity. And throughout the treatment and recovery phase, there were days when, physically, I felt just awful. It was human for me to wonder when or if I would ever get better.

It was normal to wonder if the treatments would be successful. It was perfectly understandable that I felt frightened.

Emotional and psychological distress is a real issue for those who are really sick. Forty-five percent of cancer patients, for instance, have significant mental distress.

I found that the best way to combat these natural "downers" was to keep my faith strong and my mind positive.

I never lost faith in God. The first step in recovering from a serious illness is to believe that you will get better. Better yet, the first step is to *know* that God will heal you.

I knew God would help me to recover and live to tell others. There was never a doubt in my mind. Given this faith—this knowing that God *would* make me better—I had no reason to be afraid or anxious.

Conversely, when I didn't work to keep my faith strong and my mind positive, my physical health got worse (or at least seemed to get worse) and it took me even longer to get back to normal.

My first brain surgery was much less risky and more routine that my second brain surgery. But, understandably, I was still apprehensive. When my neurologist over-medicated me on anti-seizure drugs, my mind became foggy and I was unable to think clearly. I began to worry that I had lost my brainpower—my intellect. Fear consumed me. What if I couldn't return to work? After all, I did my job with my mind—not my hands. I began to get physically worse, not better. I didn't know what was wrong with me. The stress weakened my body and I began to feel physically worse.

Finally, my neurosurgeon stepped in.

You are taking too much medicine to prevent brain seizures which no one but your neurologist seems to think you will have. I have written her several notes but she won't listen to me. My advice is for you to find a new neurologist.

I did. My new doctor gradually tapered me off anti-seizure medication, and my mind immediately starting working again. In the meantime, I had worried myself to poorer mental and physical health.

Recent studies have shown that a person's emotional and psychological well-being should be monitored during routine medical exams. As a result, doctors have started paying just as much attention to the way their patients act—their distress level—as they do to their patients' blood pressure. Some doctors have even added distress as a sixth vital sign when assessing their patients' health, along with pulse, temperature, respiration, blood pressure and pain.[3]

Because staying emotionally and spiritually positive throughout a serious illness like the ones I've had is so important, many of the chapters that follow will talk about how I kept my emotional and spiritual health strong in the wake of physical devastation.

For now, trust me. Your job is to keep your emotional health strong and your faith stronger. Prayer, fellowship, positive thinking (no stinkin' thinkin'), courage, and a strong belief that you *will* get better are all a must if you expect your physical health to improve.

THE PROCESS

"A process cannot be understood by stopping it. Understanding must move with the flow of the process, must join it and flow with it."

Frank Herbert
U.S. science fiction novelist (1920–1986)

The first time my brain bled, I was really sick. I mean really, *really* sick. I was even a little bit incoherent. And I had no idea what had happened to me. After all, I'd never had a brain hemorrhage before. Worse yet, I didn't have a clue as to what would happen next.

Throughout my illness and recovery, I felt like I was walking through a maze—not knowing what waited for me around the next turn. No one bothered to explain the "process" to me. And, as I learned by going through this repeatedly over a sixteen-year period, there *is* a process.

Most doctors and nurses are very good at the technical part of their job. Some are good at communicating their diagnosis and what the next step or two in the process will be. But few explain the entire process.

There are many reasons for this. One reason is that doctors are so specialized, several doctors may be required for you to obtain your full regiment of treatment. Your primary doctor certainly knows his job, but may, understandably, not know what the next specialist will do. Although I've seen vast improvements in doctor to patient communication since my first serious illness in 1990, it is still difficult to get them to discuss what will happen from A-Z.

The fact is, there is a distinct medical process for all illnesses. Think about a relatively minor medical illness—a respiratory infection. Many of you have had one of these. The process is as follows:

1. *Symptoms.* You experience headache, fever, sore throat, coughing up ugly yellow phlegm, or sinus/chest congestion, so you go to a doctor.

2. *Diagnosis.* The doctor asks you to describe your symptoms and how long you have been experiencing them. He performs a number of diagnostic tests on you, such as a throat culture, listening to your breathing, and taking your temperature. He concludes you have a respiratory infection.

3. *Treatment.* He prescribes antibiotics.

4. *Recovery.* You gradually get well as the antibiotics kill the germs responsible for your infection.

5. *Return to normal.* You are back to your normal self.

Does the doctor describe this process to you? Maybe yes, maybe no. But since many of you have had more than one respiratory infection in your lifetime or have known others who have had this illness, you are pretty familiar with the drill.

Can you imagine going to a doctor with a respiratory

infection, feeling just awful, and not knowing what will happen next or how long you can expect to be sick? Not knowing if you will ever be normal again? Not knowing whether you will live and, if so, what your quality of life will be?

These feelings of doubt and uncertainty are amplified with a serious illness. I have learned that just as there is a process for dealing with respiratory infections, there is also a process for dealing with more serious illnesses like brain hemorrhages.

After I had been through one bleed and one brain surgery, I learned the entire process for my condition. No one bothered to explain it to me; I just figured it out as I went along.

It is pretty standard, just like the process for a respiratory infection described above. But there are a lot more steps. Knowing what to expect in my later bleeds and surgeries helped a lot.

So here's a high-level process description of what I learned to expect when I had a brain hemorrhage.

Symptoms

My body told me when I was severely sick. This I could count on!

My brain hemorrhage symptoms included:

Severe Headache–a pounding, throbbing headache that was much worse than your everyday stress or sinus headache.

Disorientation–a feeling that I was in a fog—not all there. A spacey feeling.

Weakness–a loss of strength in my arms and legs.

Loss of neurological function–in my last episode, my face muscles stopped working—they were paralyzed. My face was droopy and I looked like I had Bell's palsy. I was unable to drink from a glass without drooling and my eye and mouth would not open or close properly. I also lost the hearing in my left ear and my left eye's vision was double and blurred.

Dizziness–severe vertigo to the point that the room was literally spinning around me.

Severe Nausea–uncontrollable vomiting.

This was my body's way of saying, "Something is not right here and you'd better stop what you are doing and get it taken care of fast–because nothing you are doing now is more important than your health!"

And the longer I ignored the symptoms, the worse they got. It was like my body was screaming at me saying, "Didn't you hear me? I told you an hour ago that something was wrong. Get yourself to a hospital or call 911!"

It is important to mention that I didn't experience all of these symptoms for all four of my brain hemorrhages. I did have a severe headache and loss of neurological function in all four. Otherwise, my symptoms varied depending on the severity and location of the bleed.

Diagnosis

I listened to my body and responded to its cry for help by going to the emergency room. The nurse put an IV into my arm and hooked me up to some equipment to monitor my blood pressure, oxygen level, and pulse.

The first doctor I saw was an emergency room trauma

doctor. She ordered blood work, x-rays, a CAT Scan, an MRI, and other diagnostic procedures to help determine what exactly was wrong with me.

Once the diagnosis was complete, the second doctor I saw was a specialist—a neurosurgeon—who consulted with me on my specific condition.

Note: For my last two bleeds, having had previous experiences with brain hemorrhages, I simply announced to the emergency room attendant upon arrival that I was having a brain hemorrhage and was able to shortcut the preliminary diagnosis step. I was admitted immediately, ahead of other patients with less serious illnesses. Similarly, if you are having severe chest pains, telling the attendant this will get you straight to the cardiology tests.

Treatment Options

My brain surgeon advised me on treatment options, including the risks and timing. For my condition, surgery is usually not recommended on a first bleed, especially if the symptoms are minor and the bleeding and swelling on the brain can be stopped with bed rest and medication. Surgery is usually recommended on a second bleed, because this particular spot now has a pattern of bleeding and successive bleeds will cause more and more nerve damage.

Whether I required surgery or not, the standard treatment was a regimen of steroids to reduce the swelling in the brain which resulted from the bleed. Even when surgery was recommended, my neurosurgeon prescribed steroids first to reduce brain swelling prior to the operation. Unless there is an eminent threat of further bleeding, it is best to wait a few weeks for the bleeding to stop and the swelling to go down prior to surgery. If there is fluid on the brain, the surgeon will drill a small hole through the skull bone and place a drain in it to allow the fluid to drain.

Intensive Care Unit

I was admitted to the hospital and, because my condition was serious, I was placed in the Intensive Care Unit (ICU) so that my condition could be monitored around the clock. Sometimes it is hard to remember that this is a good thing. But it is—you want someone monitoring your condition around the clock when you are seriously ill. Even if it means that doctors and nurses are waking you up every few hours to make sure everything is okay. And if everything is not okay, you will be moved directly to surgery.

Moving to a regular hospital room once my condition stabilized, I was moved to regular hospital room. This was also a good thing because it meant that I was no longer at high risk. It also meant that I was able to get a better (still not good) night's sleep; I was even allowed out of bed for brief times.

Treatment

For me the next steps were bed rest, steroids to keep the swelling down in my brain, and ultimately brain surgery.

Back to ICU

After surgery I was placed in ICU once again—this time surgical ICU—where my condition was monitored around the clock. Once my condition was stable, I was again moved to a regular hospital room.

Home Again

My surgeries were successful and I had no post-surgery complications so they let me go home—and yes, they kicked me
out of the hospital really quick. I spent only about five days
in the hospital, including ICU, after my two brain surgeries. I didn't feel like I was ready to go home and it took
every ounce of strength I had just to make it into the car
and then into my home. But again, home was a better place
to be than in the hospital.

Homebound

The good news was that I was home! The bad news was that
my physical condition made it impossible for me to leave
my home. It was all I could do to get up in the morning, eat
a little something, and go back to bed. This was an added
incentive for me to get better soon. I was homebound for
about six weeks. Sitting at home, staring at the walls, can
get real old really fast.

Physical, Speech, and Occupational Therapy

I started working with physical, speech, and occupational
therapists just two days after surgery while still in the hospital. Before I went home, they taught me how to walk
again—albeit with a walker. They taught me how to be as
self-sufficient as possible given my traumatized physical
condition.

Because I was homebound, these therapists continued
to work with me in my home for about six weeks until I
got strong enough to come to them. This was a good thing
because, again, I was not physically able to go to them.

Each of these therapists had their own purpose and specialty as follows:

> *Physical Therapists.* My stamina and energy had been drained by a brain hemorrhage and surgery—both of which were physical traumas to my body. I needed physical therapy like exercises and riding a stationary bike to get my strength back. My physical therapist coached me on how to ease into these exercises given my weakened condition. He also prescribed exercises designed to get my equilibrium back.

> *Occupational Therapist.* I also needed an occupational therapist for just a few days to teach me how to accomplish everyday tasks like bathing, dressing, and walking up and down stairs (just a few) while my body was beginning its healing process. I needed a walker for a while after my latest surgery and an occupational therapist taught me how to use it.

> *Speech Therapist.* My last bleed left me with facial paralysis on the left side of my face, which caused me to have difficulty speaking, eating, and closing my mouth and left eye. Not to mention the fact that it made me look funny! A speech therapist and acupuncturist were able to help me with exercises and electrical nerve stimulation.

It took me about six weeks to become physically able to leave my house. At this point, the physical and speech therapy continued for several months, but I went to them instead of them coming to me. Eventually I was able to do all my therapy on my own, without working with a therapist.

Partial Independence

I was almost completely dependent upon my wife, nurses, and other caregivers immediately after my surgery. As time passed, and as my therapists helped me improve, I was able to do more and more for myself. I remember my first few steps without a walker just a few weeks after surgery. It was a good feeling when I could begin to take care of myself again.

Full Independence

I was able to drive myself. I was able to empty the trash, lift heavy things, etc. It took me months to get to this point. After my first brain surgery, it took a full year before I could drive myself. It took a year and a half for me to feel completely normal again. With my second brain surgery, I was driving myself after only three months—but not on the freeways.

I remember the first time I drove myself after my second surgery. I announced to my wife that I was driving to the local store. Heretofore, she had chauffeured me everywhere; she looked at me like I was nuts. I said, "Don't worry honey. If I have an accident, I'll give you a call." Her reply was, "Well that makes me feel so much better!" She said this with a laugh. I remember how good it was to know I could still make her laugh.

Back to Work

At first I started working from home a little bit. Eventually I started going to the office a few hours every other day, but I stayed away from really stressful and taxing stuff. Finally, I had built up the stamina to work about twenty-five hours a week. After my first surgery, I was able to resume working full-time after about one year. My last episode sent off alarms that I was a "bleeder" and my doctor recommended that I should not return to work.

Some people have funny looking veins in the brain or spine their entire lives without any of them bleeding. After my fourth hemorrhage and second surgery, it was clear that I was not one of these people. So I am now retired.

Back to Normal—or the New Normal

It took me a year to get back to things like traveling, playing golf, driving on the freeway, or even a full day of activities. I took migraine headache medication daily for a full year. In other words, it took me a full year to get back to normal.

But even then, it was a different normal. The trauma of enduring a serious illness took a toll on me. Headaches were an every day occurrence for months. And then there was my physical body, which, although repaired, was not the same. I still have some residual nerve damage from my last surgery—but this is now my *new normal*.

The medical system has a process to get you from that first trip to the emergency room or doctor's office to wellness. The problem is that most medical professionals don't share that process with their patients. Many patients, like me, often feel as though they are feeling their way through a maze, never knowing what's around the next corner. I found that recovering from my illnesses was much easier when I knew what was about to happen to me and when it would happen.

I recommend you talk with your doctor and ask him

or her to explain your "process" to you. The doctor's initial reaction might be, "let's just take it one step at a time," or "everyone is different and it will depend on your specific situation." But, if you are like me, and you want to know what to expect, press your doctor to give you an average scenario—at least a high-level overview of what is likely to happen to you. The doctor should know what is going to happen over the next month or two.

LISTEN TO YOUR BODY

"God gave us two ears but only one mouth so we can listen twice as much as we talk."

Unknown

Your body is a wonderful communicator when you get sick. When you get really sick, your body screams at you telling you that something is horribly wrong. You have a high fever, an excruciating headache, unbearable pain, severe nausea, etc. This is your body's way of telling you to seek help.

Do you listen? Unfortunately the answer too many times is no. We dismiss these internal cries for help as nothing. We tell ourselves that, whatever it is, it will pass in a few days or a few weeks.

Don't procrastinate. When your body lets you know you are sick, seek immediate medical attention—the sooner the better. Listen to your body! What is the worst thing that can happen?

On the one hand, your doctor could tell you there is nothing seriously wrong. While it may be embarrassing to rush to your doctor's office or local emergency room believing you have a serious illness, only to be told that you are fine, it is good news and it is nice to know.

On the other hand, your doctor may tell you that something is critically wrong and that you need immediate attention. In talking to other patients, I can tell you that this is the reason why many people don't seek immediate attention for an illness sooner rather than later—they simply don't want to hear bad news.

I hope you know how silly this is. The longer you wait, the worse the illness will get, and the tougher it will be to get well. In my case, I knew immediately when I had a brain hemorrhage.

Except in the case of my first hemorrhage. The first time my brain bled, I didn't know what had happened, but my body told me that whatever was going on was serious. I felt and acted as though I was suffering from a stroke. I couldn't walk without assistance. I couldn't dress myself. My head was pounding, causing horrible pain. But I was young, in a foreign country, and pretty cocky about my physical health. So I did something really stupid—I waited five days to see a doctor, hoping I would improve on my own.

Doctors made house calls in this foreign country. I was physically unable to get to the emergency room, and I never even considered an ambulance—don't ask me why. So I called the doctor to my house. He told me he didn't believe anything was seriously wrong with me (boy, was he wrong!) but recommended that I see an ear, nose, and throat (ENT) specialist to see what was causing my acute vertigo (dizziness).

But what about this pounding headache? What about the fact that I don't have the strength to walk up a flight of stairs?

What about the tingling in my left arm and leg? He didn't know—but the ENT doctor was the best place to start.

Let me pause here and say how thankful we should all be for living in the United States of America where we can receive quality medical care. I saw a lot of supposed specialists in the foreign country where I was living and none of them diagnosed my condition. I received no treatment; no steroids, no hospitalization, no MRI—nothing. I saw a different doctor every time I went to the hospital. So I started over again with a new doctor every week. Each of them had a different opinion—none of which had anything to do with my brain. This was socialized medicine at its worse.

Three months passed before I was physically able to go outside my home. In the meantime, I listened to my body. It continued to tell me that I was really sick. It told me I should stay home and in bed, so I did. When I attempted to lie on my left side or my back, the headache pain became excruciating; when I shifted back to my right side, the pain got better. I quickly learned that my body was telling me to lie on my right side, and I did.

My first brain hemorrhage went undiagnosed and I gradually got better. I healed and got back to normal—not because of any medical treatments I received—by listening to my body.

My condition was not diagnosed until eighteen months later when my second brain hemorrhage occurred in the same location. By this time I was back in the United States. I went to the doctor with weakness in my arms and legs. I also told her about my earlier health problems while living abroad. Finally, I told her that I thought there was something wrong with my brain. This is what my body was telling me.

I had told the doctors abroad the same thing and they brushed it off. I kept saying over and over again that whatever happened to me had something to do with my brain—they continued to treat me for acute vertigo and potential heart problems and a variety of other conditions, none of which were pertinent.

My doctor in the United States was much less skeptical, and she agreed to send me for a CT scan and an MRI.

The very next day I got a panicked call from the doctor's office directing me to come back immediately. They showed me the MRI and dried, spattered blood covered the entire right side of my brain. They surmised that most of the blood was from a brain bleed eighteen months earlier. But there was also some fresh blood from a more recent bleed. Two weeks later I had brain surgery. Given the amount of dried blood, I was told that I should feel lucky to have survived the bleed eighteen months earlier. I was told I was lucky to be alive!

I listened to my body. My body had been telling me for eighteen months that something was wrong with my brain. I asked the doctor to explore this possibility and, fortunately, she did.

In reflecting back, I know I survived that first episode abroad through the grace of God and by listening to my body. I remember lying for days with the right side of my head on the pillow. My body told me that laying on my right side was the right thing to do because, when I did this, the excruciating headache got better. It turns out that lying on my right side put needed pressure on the hemorrhage, which, combined with the bed rest my body told me to impose on myself, helped stop the bleeding and probably saved my life. My body—not the doctors—had told me what to do. All I had to do was listen.

After all four of my brain hemorrhages and both of my brain surgeries, my body has also told me what foods to eat. My body craved certain foods after each of my episodes. These cravings were for foods I enjoy but rarely ate and they were the same cravings in all four cases.

I craved fish, especially salmon—canned salmon, baked salmon, grilled salmon, smoked salmon, salmon Alexander—my body craved any kind of salmon. I wanted to eat salmon for every meal—breakfast, lunch, and dinner.

I know retrospectively that my body was telling me that salmon would help my brain heal. I have since learned that salmon is good food for your brain, however, I also know that salmon contains a high amount of omega-3 fatty acids, which thin the blood. Thus I didn't eat salmon (and other blood thinning foods) until my doctor told me that my bleeding had stopped, and I limited my consumption to once a day for a few weeks.

I craved spinach, asparagus, and broccoli. I ate spinach, asparagus, and broccoli four or five times a week, sometimes as a snack and sometimes along with my salmon. These foods contain high amounts of Vitamin K, a substance that helps clot the blood.

There are worse things to crave, like milkshakes. I drank a huge milkshake every day for about a month after each of my episodes. Not one of those fast food restaurant milkshakes, but one made at home, in the blender with real ice cream, real milk, and real fruit. And when I say huge, I'm talking about thirty-six ounces each. My body told me that banana milkshakes would be especially helpful. I'm not sure why.

The funny thing about these cravings is that once things healed, the cravings went away. My body was telling me that these things were going to help me get better and I listened. When I didn't need them any longer, my body stopped craving them.

While we're on the topic of nutrition, let me say that another thing I learned was to throw my diet out the window while my body was telling me to eat salmon, milkshakes, and bananas. I have battled a life-long weight problem, but my body was telling me that my weight was the last thing I needed to be concerned about when recuperating from a brain hemorrhage or brain surgery.

My body told me I needed bed rest and sleep—an unbelievable amount of sleep. Immediately after both of my surgeries and all of my hemorrhages, I slept a lot. I would go to bed at 7:00 or 8:00 pm and sleep until 8:00 am the next day. I got up, struggled to shower, shave, and brush my teeth. Then I went back to bed until breakfast was ready. In the early days, I sat in a recliner to eat my breakfast, but as soon as I was physically stronger, I sat at the kitchen table. Then I went back to bed for an hour or so. I got up for lunch then took a two-hour nap in the afternoon. Then I struggled to make it to 7:00 pm or 8:00 pm when I went to bed for the night.

By my count, I spent seventeen hours a day in bed, most of it sleeping. Physically, this is what my body was telling me I needed to do. Of course, as soon as my body told me it was stronger, I began to cut down my sleeping time and today I sleep the normal eight hours per night—that's it.

As I have mentioned before, my left eye was damaged

as a result of my fourth brain hemorrhage. The vision in this eye was blurry and double. I also couldn't close it all the way. The combination of these conditions made my eye easily strained. I could only read or watch television for a few minutes at a time. Even then, the damage to my left eye meant that I was primarily using my right eye to see.

I asked several doctors what I should do about this left eye. Should I attempt to use it, even though it wasn't working correctly, or should I rest it waiting for the damaged nerves to heal?

I didn't really get an answer to this question, so I listened to my body. My body told me to use my left eye as much as I could bear it—no matter how painful it was. I bought an eye patch and placed it over my right eye, forcing me to try to see things out of the left eye. I did some muscle exercises—which I invented—to strengthen muscles around the left eye. And, I prayed a lot that God would help me to see again out of my left eye; instinctively I knew that of all the things that were wrong with me, my vision was the most important to get back.

At first this was all very difficult. Staring at the blurry television image with only my left eye was physically painful. But, in the end, the vision in my left eye was one of the first things to heal. My body had told me to do the right thing and thankfully I listened.

Your body will tell you when you are really sick. Your body will often tell you what is wrong with you, even before a doctor makes his diagnosis. My body also told me what foods to eat to assist in my recovery, how much rest to get, and when to resume normal activities. It is important to listen to your body.

THE WORD

> "The ultimate measure of a man is not where he stands in moments of comfort and convenience, but where he stands at times of challenge and controversy."
>
> Martin Luther King, Jr.

Your body tells you that something is seriously wrong with you and, if you are not too macho—or macho-ess—you listen to your body and go to a doctor for help.

After examining you and running a few tests, your doctor may speculate about what is wrong; but most likely, he will refer you to a specialist who is more knowledgeable about patients with your specific condition. It will probably be this specialist who gives you the *word*—the diagnosis.

Several words, when uttered by doctors, have the ability to incite absolute panic and fear in people. "You have cancer...you have liver disease...you have AIDS...you have a heart problem." Or in my case, "you have a brain hemorrhage."

No matter how much I knew that I *might* get news like this, it was still a shock. One minute I felt great. Life was good! I was in good health. The next minute my world was literally turned upside down. Things that I had considered to be important were suddenly put on hold while I attempted to make some sense of what was happening to me.

I remember the first time a doctor told me that I had had a brain hemorrhage. It is impossible to describe the emptiness and hurt of that moment. I felt as if I was in a dream. It was the last thing I expected to hear, even though I instinctively knew there was something wrong with my brain.

I went through this several times, but I never got used to hearing the doctor say those words. "You've had a brain hemorrhage." Even worse was hearing the doctor say, "You will require brain surgery."

By the way, it is a good idea to take someone with you (friend, relative, spouse, etc.) on these early visits, because chances are that you won't hear much past the diagnosis. You will receive other critical information during this first visit, and, someone needs to hear what else the doctor has to say!

After the first time or two, I would arrive at the emergency room and announce to the attendant at the main desk, "I am having a brain hemorrhage." But even when I knew what was wrong with me, I would still get that sinking feeling when the doctor confirmed it. It just caused me to feel immediately anxious, worked up, nervous, and worried.

I've found, by talking with others, that all of these feelings are normal. The body has a built in defense mechanism that causes adrenaline to be produced in huge quantities when it senses danger. It's called the flight or fight mechanism. It literally makes your body feel like fleeing or fighting the bad news.

The question is, are you going to fly away and try to escape your illness or are you going to stand your ground and put up a good fight? Sooner or later you will sort things out and conclude that it is time for you to fight the best fight ever.

Adding to the stress is the fact that some doctors are not particularly good at delivering the news. They just blurt it out as though it was a routine daily thing—which for some it is.

No matter how delicately (or not) my doctor delivered the word, I always told him that I was frightened, because I was. My doctors probably already knew this, but me telling them straight forwardly gave them an opportunity to respond. I mostly got immediate positive feedback from them, such as:

- This is very operable.

- I have done dozens of these procedures before with great success. I expect yours will be equally successful.

- I believe it is unlikely that we will cause any collateral damage during the operation (additional nerve damage while attempting to remove the source of the bleeding via surgery).

- I am going to keep you in the hospital under close scrutiny until we're sure you are out of danger.

- If you are interested, I can arrange for you to talk to some of my other patients with similar conditions and hear, firsthand, how well they are doing.

- We can arrange for the hospital chaplain to visit you today, if you would like.

Words such as these, coming from your doctor, can have a great calming effect.

Knowing that most patients with your condition survive and go on to lead normal lives is a good thing. Too often we hear of those who don't survive; but with the help of modern medicine, more and more people with serious illnesses are being treated successfully. Keep this *calming thought* in mind when you get the word!

And listen to your doctor. He will probably give you some advice about how to make sure you don't get worse before he can make you better. In my case, I was confined to bed for five days to stop the bleeding. When I was released from the hospital, and waiting for my surgery date, I was cautioned not to lift heavy objects, not to overexert myself (not that I was able), and to stay away from work. "Don't do anything to raise your blood pressure," the doctors said. "And, if you notice further neurological deterioration, come to the emergency room immediately."

Brain hemorrhages cause swelling in the brain. This must be stopped to avoid further nerve damage. And it is best that the swelling is gone before surgery is done. My doctor put me on a four-week regimen of steroids—not the body building kind—to reduce the swelling.

Steroids make me extremely hyperactive and anxious. I was already anxious and the steroids amplified this almost to the point of being unbearable. Apparently they don't affect everyone this way, but this is the affect they have on me. In the first week or so, I had to wake up in the middle of the night to take them.

Being extremely anxious and setting my alarm for 2:00 a.m. every night was not pleasant, but I took the medicine religiously. I hated it, but I did what the doctor told me to do.

In summary, getting the word—the diagnosis—of a serous illness is understandably frightening. Tell your doctor that you are afraid and allow him to provide some reassuring words. Although some illnesses can't be treated, you will probably find that many patients with your illness have survived and gone on to live active lives. Seize on this positive thought. Follow your doctor's orders. Take the prescribed medications and adhere to the prescribed advice to make sure you don't get worse before she or he can make you better.

HIRE AN *EXCEPTIONAL* DOCTOR

"My philosophy is that not only are you responsible for your life, but doing the best at this
moment puts you in the best place the next
moment."

Oprah Winfrey
U.S. actress and television talk show host

For heaven's sake, if you are diagnosed with a serious illness—unless you are in an immediate life or death situation—don't just go to the local emergency room, pull the
specialist on-call for that day, and proceed with treatment.
Do your research, conduct some interviews, and then
hire the doctor that is most qualified to treat your specific
condition.

My father use to tell me that 50% of all doctors graduated in the bottom half of their class. True. So, the way I
see it, there are good doctors, there are great doctors, and
then there are *exceptional* doctors. My goal was to get an

exceptional doctor. The doctor that was the best qualified to treat my specific condition. After all, I deserved the best! This should be your attitude as well.

A friend was recently diagnosed with a tumor on the side of his brain, just above the left ear. He was advised to have surgery because of the risk that the tumor might grow and cause him to lose his hearing. Apparently his mother and uncle had a similar condition that had caused them to lose their hearing. After surgery he wasn't doing well.

Collateral damage during surgery had caused him to lose his hearing. It had also caused him severe balance and speech problems. I was told that his surgery was done in Miami, Florida. "Why Miami?" I asked. A mutual friend replied, "Because that is where he lived." Wrong answer. Maybe there was an exceptional neurosurgeon in Miami who was experienced with dealing with this condition, but maybe he could have done even better had he looked more broadly.

Depending upon your condition, you may have to look all over the world to find the most exceptional doctor. The best doctor may be in a larger city, at a top-notch teaching facility, in another state, or they may be in Europe or Asia. Wherever that doctor resides, you need to find him or her.

When my mother, who lives in Kansas, suffered her first hemorrhage, she sought help from doctors where she lived—in the small mid-western city of Wichita with a population of about 350,000.

Twelve months passed and the neurosurgeon in her hometown did not diagnose her condition, let alone treat the illness. My mother gradually got worse and worse as the bleeding continued and the nerve damage progressed.

Finally she made an appointment at the Mayo Clinic

in Rochester, Minnesota. The clinic put her through an exhaustive set of tests and within just a few days they had diagnosed the problem—a cavernous angioma bleed in her spine. Yes, this *is* a genetic thing.

By then, it was too late. Although surgery was performed, her condition continued to worsen and today she is in a wheelchair, unable to care for herself. Her left leg is paralyzed and she is in constant pain. And she has other permanent neurological problems.

In retrospect, had she sought help outside of Wichita sooner, her condition probably would have been diagnosed and treated sooner, and she would have had a better chance to recover fully.

Similarly, a friend of mine was recently diagnosed with cancer and is undergoing chemo and radiation therapy. She began by visiting a doctor in a small town complaining of severe pain in her legs. Unfortunately, it took several weeks for this small-town doctor to make a full diagnosis of bone and lung cancer. In the meantime, she lost precious time before transferring to a prestigious teaching hospital about an hour from her home where she is now receiving the proper care.

My last brain hemorrhage was in the pons area of my brain stem. This is the most critical area of the brain for surgery—the most difficult area to perform surgery. As my neurosurgeon told me, "every millimeter counts." Only a handful of doctors in the country are qualified to perform such an operation. The first three neurosurgeons I talked to wouldn't even consider performing the surgery, because it was just too risky. These doctors, and most other neurosurgeons, don't have the skill or experience to attempt surgery in this critical part of the brain.

So I began to look for an *exceptional* doctor who *was* trained and qualified to operate on me—a doctor who had successfully done this operation again and again. I knew from researching my previous bleeds that one of these neurosurgeons was in Phoenix, Arizona. I was surprised to find that there was another qualified neurosurgeon in Dallas, Texas, where I was living. I chose the doctor in Dallas.

How did I find my *exceptional* doctor—the one eminently qualified to perform my surgery? I talked with other doctors. My first neurosurgeon told me he was, personally, not qualified and referred me to Doctor Spetzler in Phoenix.

In the meantime, I was moved to a different hospital, and the second neurosurgeon also told me, "You definitely need to have surgery, but I am not qualified to perform this procedure." I simply asked this guy, "Who *is* best qualified to do it?" He told me that either Doctor Spetzler in Phoenix or Doctor White in Dallas specialized in my specific condition.

I also did some research myself—on the Internet. I decided that the fact there was a doctor in Dallas who specialized in doing brain surgery on the brain stem was divine.

So, I interviewed this neurosurgeon (from my hospital bed). After all, I was about to hire this guy to open my head up and remove some nasty veins from my brain. This was the most important employee I would ever hire. I asked him questions such as:

Question: If you were in my shoes, who would you have do the surgery?

Answer: Either myself or Dr. Spetzler in Phoenix.

Question: Are you as good as or better than Dr. Spetzler? Why?

Answer: We are both excellent doctors with training and experience operating on vascular problems in the brainstem. I happen to think I'm a little better. But, then again, he would probably say that he is a little better.

Question: How many surgeries in the pons area of the brainstem have you done? How many of these have been successful?

Answer: This is my specialty and so I have done many. All have been successful. I believe your condition is very operable or I wouldn't recommend or attempt surgery.

Question: Will you use a laser knife or will this be an invasive surgery?

Answer: Laser knives are not effective for patients with your condition, so this will be an invasive procedure.

Thought: Ouch!

Question: Will you be operating under a microscope?

Answer: Yes—this is a very delicate procedure that requires microscopic accuracy.

Question: How soon will you be able to do the operation? (I wanted to get it over with!)

Answer: As soon as possible. As soon as we're sure the swelling has gone down and the bleeding has stopped.

Question: What will my recovery time be?

Answer: Although every patient is different, I would estimate three to six months.

Reflection: In three months, I was able to do many things.

In six months, I was able to do more. But it took a year for me to feel normal again.

Question: Will the surgery make my droopy face, blindness, hearing, and balance better?

Answer: No, surgery will not improve any nerve damage already caused by your hemorrhage. In fact, surgery will temporarily make you feel even worse.

Question: Will anything make my droopy face, blindness, hearing, and balance better?

Answer: Damaged nerves can heal over time. Each patient is different. Your nerve damage is in the pons area of the brainstem and it will be more difficult to achieve healing because of the serious location of the bleed. But, we will do everything we can in terms of post-surgery therapy to help.

Thought: Bring on the therapy! I'm going to beat this thing.

Question: Will you perform the surgery alone, or will residents and other doctors be sharing the work?

Answer: No resident will touch the knife. I will be doing the surgery. However, I will call on a skull bone specialist to help get us through the skull bone—he's the best at this.

Question: So you are telling me that the surgery will not help restore my nerve damage and it will even make me feel temporarily worse. Why should I have this surgery?

Answer: Once a cavernous angioma has bled, it is more likely to bleed again in the future. Each bleed will cause progressively more and more nerve damage. Removing

*it is the only way to insure that you don't get worse. And
with therapy you may get better.*

Thought: *May get better? No way. I will get better!*

Question: What are the risks of surgery?

Answer: *I won't kid you. This is a very delicate place to
operate. Every millimeter counts. But your defective
vein is near the surface and I believe we can remove it
without causing collateral (additional) nerve damage.*

Question: What is the risk of not having the surgery?

Answer: *Unless we remove this particular vein, it will probably bleed again and again, and each recurrence will
cause additional nerve damage. Eventually the damage
will be irreversible.*

Thought: *I've seen this firsthand with my mother. I don't
want to end up paralyzed and in a wheel chair like my
mother.*

I asked him these questions and more. I was impressed that
he had the patience and took the time to answer each one
of them. This gave me confidence that I would get his time
and attention later on in the process. He was impressed
that I asked so many good questions and that I was knowledgeable about my condition. When we finished I think we
both felt good about what each of us were doing.

Nonetheless, I got a second opinion from someone
else I trusted. It was quite easy to do. I paid for copies
of my MRIs out of my own pocket (they weren't cheap)
and shipped them overnight to Dr. Mario Zucarello at the
University Hospital in Cincinnati. I knew Dr. Zucarello
because he had operated on my son two years earlier. Dr.
Zucarello called me the next day to say he concurred with

Dr. White's diagnosis and his recommendation for surgery. He also told me that he knew of Dr. White and that I was in good hands.

Just to make sure, I simultaneously sent another copy of my films to Dr. Yoshiro Takaoka, the surgeon who did my first brain operation in Cleveland, Ohio. He also concurred with Dr. White's diagnosis and recommendation.

Dr. Zucarello and Dr. Takaoka were people I knew and trusted and it was important for me to check with them and obtain their advice. By the way, they both called me back, personally, to talk with me about my decision.

My advice: Unless you are in an immediate life or death situation, always seek a second opinion. In fact some medical insurance companies may require you to get a second opinion before you undergo risky surgery or some other serious treatment.

Don't be timid about changing doctors until you get to someone who can best help you. I mentioned earlier that my original brain hemorrhage went undiagnosed while I was living abroad. British Petroleum, the company I was working for, offered to fly me back to the Cleveland Clinic in the United States to make sure I got the care I needed. This was my chance to get back to the United States where I could get a higher quality of medical treatment and a chance to get a proper diagnosis.

But I turned them down. I assumed that if there were something wrong with me, surely one of the doctors in England would have diagnosed it. I was also physically weak and couldn't imagine taking a transcontinental flight back to the States.

In retrospect, that was pretty stupid of me. I just didn't want to start over again with a new regimen of doctors.

But, what I failed to realize was that I was making no progress with the current regimen of doctors. I learned from this experience. Now, if I'm not making progress with my current doctor(s), I change to someone who can make progress.

Next, I did some research on the hospital where the surgery would take place and where I would be treated before and after surgery. I talked to friends and co-workers. It was amazing how many of them knew firsthand about Zale-Lipshy hospital (part of the outstanding teaching medical facilities at the University of Texas Southwest Hospital). I was amazed that even my pastor had his knee replacement done at Zale-Lipshy. I found that it had an excellent reputation for its quality of care, its service-oriented attitude, and its individual attention to each patient. And, because it was a prestigious teaching hospital, it had a well-deserved reputation for being on the leading edge of the most recent medical procedures, being able to treat conditions that most other hospitals were not yet able to address.

By the time I got to my surgery date, I had done extensive research on my neurosurgeon, my condition, and the hospital where I would be having the surgery. Actually, I wasn't able to do *all* the research. My youngest son helped a lot.

I sought out patient references and I talked to other doctors. I consulted with friends both inside and outside the medical community. I interviewed my prospective neurosurgeon, having changed doctors three times (to get to that *exceptional* doctor I needed) and I got a second opinion from my son's neurosurgeon in Cincinnati.

So, by the time my surgery date came, I was at peace. I

was mentally convinced that I was doing the right thing. I was confident that:

- Surgery was the right option for me—even risky surgery
- I had the right doctor for my specific condition
- I was going to the right medical facility

It was very important to me that I felt good about my decision to have surgery, my choice of doctor, and his choice of medical facilities. I made an agreement with myself that no matter what happened, I wouldn't second-guess my decision.

Later, when my nerve-damaged left eye needed attention, I received follow-up surgery and treatment from a neruo-ophthalmologist, one of five such specialists in the state of Texas, and exactly the kind of specialist required for my condition.

Interview and choose your doctor—don't let the system choose one for you. Your doctor works for you—you don't work for your doctor. Make sure you hire an *exceptional* doctor to treat your illness. After all, you are literally placing your life in this person's hands. He or she is now your most important employee! Interview, do your research, and make yourself comfortable with your choice.

And, don't be afraid to get a second opinion or even switch doctors if that is what it takes to reassure you that you are in the right hands.

GET YOUR PERSONAL AFFAIRS IN ORDER

"In time, it isn't the things you do, but the things you leave undone, which gives you heartache at the setting of the Sun."

Anonymous

A serious illness, especially one that requires major surgery, will take you out of commission for a while. There is even the possibility that you will die. It is important that your spouse, children, and others be able to carry on with business even if you can't.

This is a delicate topic to address, but one that absolutely must be addressed. Try looking at it this way: by getting your personal affairs in order before you begin treatments, you can relieve a great burden from your family and bring yourself the peace of mind that comes from knowing that you and your family are prepared.

For my first brain surgery, I was totally unprepared. I had no last will and testimony. I had no medical power of attorney. My wife didn't know what my wishes were, should I die or become incapacitated. Worse yet, I didn't even know that these were important issues. I was focused on the fact that someone was getting ready to cut my brain open—I was focused on me and what was about to happen to me.

My boss at work told me that I needed to get this done. He told me that a friend of his had died and had left no instructions or preferences. So on top of his family having to deal with his demise, they also had to deal with the ensuing search for important documents, some of which didn't exist. They also had to deal with guessing what his choices would have been had he taken the time to document them. This made the situation even worse. He simply said to me, "Les, you need to get your personal affairs in order now!" He even offered our corporate legal and human resource departments' help if I desired. It was the best advice I ever received.

This need not be a scary or depressing process. After all, death is inevitable—hopefully not now—but sooner or later everyone dies. Think about your family. Do it for them. Do you really want them to try to do deal with losing you while at the same time dealing with the stress and uncertainty brought on by the lack of written instructions on your wishes? Do you really want them searching the house and every bank in town for important documents? The answer is no.

The best time to take care of matters is when you are well. Unfortunately most of us don't do this when we are well. We have a hundred excuses. We're too busy. We're in perfect health. We're too young to be concerned about wills and medical powers of attorney. We dislike lawyers and don't want to deal with them, especially on matters like this. We don't want to spend the money. I could go on and on. I have four words for those of *us* who haven't dealt with these matters when well—get on with it! Ever since my first brain surgery, I have made it a point to keep my personal affairs current and I have made sure that my wife and sons know where important documents are stashed.

If you haven't taken care of things before you're diagnosed with a serious illness, do it right away. Don't let the process make you morbid, scared, or worried. Don't let the process overwhelm you because it involves lawyers. Rather, think of it as lifting a giant weight from your family and friends, should the worst happen. Getting your personal affairs in order should reassure you that everything will be okay. This should give you both peace of mind and a sense of accomplishment.

If you don't have a lawyer, someone from social services at the hospital can help you locate one that specializes in estate planning. You have taken good care of your family through the years so there should be no excuse for not taking care of them now.

So what exactly do you need to do? I've already mentioned that you need a last will and testament and a medical power of attorney. Your last will and testament is a legal document that tells the courts how you want your property distributed should you die. It also names someone to be the executor of your estate. This could be a brother, sister, friend, or family member. For instance, it is common for a parent to pick an adult son or daughter as their executor. A will may also contain things like where you wish to be buried, who you would prefer to deliver your eulogy, whether you want to be cremated or not, and even what hymns would like sung at your funeral. You can even designate who gets custody of your cat or dog. A last will and testament can literally be used to document any postmortem wishes or desires.

You will also want a medical power of attorney. This will allow you to designate a close friend or family member who can make medical decisions on your behalf should you be unable to do so yourself. Simple things such as whether a doctor can run a test while you are under anesthesia can become much more complicated without this simple document. In my case, my wife, Sharon, has the power to make any and all medical decisions on my behalf.

But you need to go further. Make sure that your spouse or someone else you trust knows where these documents are located. If possible, make sure they are on file at the hospital immediately after you are admitted—before treatments begin.

Make sure this same spouse or someone you trust knows the location of any life insurance policies, bank statements, birth and marriage certificates, 401k and IRA information, other important papers (such as your social security card), the deed to your home, and the title for your car or truck. Should you have any outstanding loans for your home, car, boat, etc., make sure someone knows about them. If you have purchased a cemetery plot or made other pre-arrangements for your funeral, let them be known as well.

And if any of these documents are in a safety deposit box, please make sure someone—your spouse, a close family member, the executor of your estate, or your lawyer— knows the name and address of the financial institution where the box is located. Double check that someone has a key to this box with the right to access it without you being there.

Another personal matter that needs to be dealt with

is your employment status. Check to see when or if your company will place you on disability, retirement status, workers compensation, etc. Determine what monies will come in from these sources and then make sure your spouse and loved ones are aware of the situation. When I worked for British Petroleum, it took me a full year to recover from my first brain hemorrhage. Fortunately, British Petroleum's benefits plan provided me with full disability benefits throughout this entire year. My last job provided similar benefits.

And equally important as all these papers and legal stuff, make sure that everyone you are close to knows how much you love them. Tell your children how proud you are of them. Tell your spouse how much you have valued their love and companionship. Let your boss know how grateful you are for everything he did for you. Let everyone you care about know how much he or she means to you. Do it for them as well as yourself.

The most common regret that I've heard from survivors of someone who has passed away is that they didn't get a chance to tell them how much they loved them. I suspect that if we were able to talk to the deceased, they would say the same thing. Make it easy and take the first step. Just say, "I love you very much." And the likely response will be, "I love you too."

So get your personal affairs in order—not for your sake but for the sake of your loved ones. Don't make it a morbid process. Tell yourself that death is inevitable and that this is a task that needs to be done sooner or later. It will give you the peace of mind that comes from knowing that you have spared your family from the stress that comes from making choices about your desires because you have clearly documented these in advance. And you have spared your family from searching for documents because you will have told them where to look in advance.

SET UP A COMMUNICATION CHAIN

"This 'telephone' has too many shortcomings to be seriously considered as a means of communication. The device is inherently of no value to us."

Western Union internal memo, 1876

Your illness affects you dramatically. But don't forget that it also affects your friends, family, co-workers, your clergy, and many others you are close to. They, in-turn, will tell *their* friends and family about you and, before you know it, folks you have never even met will be praying for you, concerned about you, and interested in your progress. There could be hundreds of good-hearted people who will be anxious to hear how you are doing!

These people will want to know the results of your medical tests and doctors visits, whether surgery or some other treatment is required, the results of treatments, the outcome of surgeries, and your progress toward recovery—

even the little steps forward. In short, they will be hungry for information about your illness.

Before the Internet and email, it would have been nearly impossible to keep these hundreds of folks up-to-date and informed. But with email and group mailing lists, it is relatively easy. And a short email will help keep the phone from ringing off the hook—because if they don't hear from you they will probably call to find out what is going on.

I strongly recommend you create a communication chain. Send a periodic update to friends, neighbors, etc. via email. A weekly update has worked for me. When something special happens mid-week, don't hesitate to send another update. These friends and neighbors will then forward it to their friends and neighbors, and all those who are deeply concerned about your condition will be kept up-to-date.

During the first weeks of my illnesses, I was unable to send updates myself, so my wife, Sharon, composed and sent them. She would send a weekly email every Monday morning. One of the people on her mailing list was my assistant at work. My assistant would forward Sharon's message to the 4,000 employees in the company I worked for, as well as business associates from outside the company. My wife's message also went to a few close friends from church, which in turn forwarded it to other church members who had placed me on their prayer list—and so on and so forth. The following is a sample of an update my wife sent just two weeks after my last hemorrhage.

Dear Friends,

Les continues to improve. The swelling has gone down in his brain and the bleeding has stopped. He had a gold band surgically implanted in this left eyelid so he can now close his eye most of the way. I have started calling him Golden Eye.

We do not have a date for brain surgery yet and this has both of us a little anxious. We call the doctor's office daily, but keep getting the same answer—we're working on it. Naturally we both want it to happen sooner rather than later.

He is watching a little bit of TV and listening to books on tape. It is difficult for him to watch TV or read books because the vision in his left eye is still blurred and double. He wears a "pirate's patch" over that eye, on occasion, to keep it from getting too strained.

He appreciates all the get-well cards, flowers, plants, and gifts that so many of you have sent. He really brightens up when they come. And, thanks to you, they come daily.

Many of you have asked about visiting. He is just too weak and tired to accept visitors right now, but we will continue to keep in touch.

His outlook continues to be positive and he is confident that he will recover fully from this episode. Every so often I have to remind him that it takes time and patience.

Love,
Sharon

As soon as I was able, I began composing and sending my own weekly email updates. This meant a lot to those who were following my progress. It had been weeks since many of them had seen me or heard from me. Hearing directly from me reassured them that I was on the mend.

This is an example of one of my first emails after I had recovered enough to do my own thing.

Hi everyone.

I know Sharon has been sending weekly updates to you. I just wanted you to hear from me directly now that I am able.

First of all, thanks to all of you for your prayers. I can't tell you how much this has meant to me. Because of your prayers I am on the road to recovery and have the strength to bear the burden.

Second, thanks for all the cards, letters, gifts, flowers, plants, etc. I wish you could all see our house. It looks like a flower and gift shop. It makes me feel so good that you are thinking of me.

I continue to get better. Something really great happened this week. I was talking on my cell phone using my good, right ear when our home phone rang. It was Sharon who had run to the store, so I instinctively picked it up and put it to my bad, left ear. Last week I was completely deaf in the left ear, but this week I was able to hear Sharon's voice when she called. I was overjoyed! The hearing is not all the way back, and her voice was muffled, but I have made huge progress.

You will hear from me again next week.

Les

Another approach to sharing information about your progress is to use the Internet. Some friends of mine recently gave birth to twin girls. One of these beautiful babies has a partial clef lip and palate—not that they didn't already have their hands full. In addition to the twins they have been blessed with two boys, aged three and five. These are really great folks and a lot of people are concerned about them and what is happening.

They are using CarePages.com to post photos, messages, and status updates with anyone who logs into their

CarePage. According to their website, "CarePages are free, personal, private Web pages that help family and friends communicate when someone is facing illness." It is a great website, and it will cost you nothing. It allows friends and acquaintances to retrieve information at their leisure rather than having information pushed at them via email. These same people can also post messages of support, encouragement, and prayer. Check it out.

An email or the Internet are good, efficient ways to keep in touch with most of those who are concerned, and it will be a good tool for most people and events. However, there are some people that you will want to make more personal contact with via telephone. Your closest friends, your parents, children, and closest family members fall into this category. Perhaps your pastor and other friends from church will also appreciate a more personal contact. And when a special event occurs, such as surgery, you will want to reach out to as many people as possible immediately.

When my surgeries were performed, my family and friends made calls as soon as there was news to let everyone know how things had gone. Again, there were just too many people for one person to contact quickly. So my wife made a telephone communication chain. She made a list of names and numbers and divided it up between my sons (who had made the trip from Ohio to Texas to be with us during surgery) and herself. We told each of these folks in advance that they would get a call from Sharon, Dave, Doug, or Mike as soon as they knew something. We also asked them to contact a few more people and so on. In a matter of about thirty minutes, hundreds of people knew that my surgery had gone well.

Now, my last surgery was very risky, given the location of my bleed. I had suffered severe nerve damage. And, there was a risk that the surgery would result in collateral damage—additional, unintentional damage to other neurological functions. This was well known by everyone on our communication chain.

Establish a communication chain. A lot of people will want to know how you are doing. Email and the Internet are great for communicating to the masses, but be sure someone makes a more personal call to close friends and relatives. A lot of people will want to do something to help during your illness. Assigning them a role in the communication chain is a good way to take them up on their offer.

SO, HOW ARE YOU DOING?

> "A bore is a man who when you ask him how he is, tells you."
>
> Bert Leston Taylor
> *The So-Called Human Race* (1922)

During the course of my illness, many friends and family asked me how things were going. At first they made inquiries over the telephone or via email. When I was well enough to accept visitors (and I recommend you do this as soon as possible), they began asking me directly, "So, how are you doing?" This was a difficult question for me to answer, especially when I felt really bad.

I came to realize that no matter how I felt, the correct answer was something positive like "good, better, or improving." An even better answer was "great!" And I said it with enthusiasm. Or better yet I said, "Great, thanks to your prayers."

Unacceptable answers were, "I feel lousy, terrible, or bored." Also unacceptable was anything that intimated that I felt dreadful. It wasn't good for me, or the person who asked the question, to pour out my problems. They would no doubt feel sad or stunned. And, I really didn't want to drag my friends, co-workers, and family members down.

From my perspective I needed to reinforce in my mind that the glass was half full—not half empty. I needed to convince myself that things would improve. The mind is a funny thing—it will believe that things are good if you say they are good, over and over again. Remember, the first step in getting well is to *know* that you *will* get well.

I tried to place myself in the shoes of the person who asked the question. Did they want to know all the gory details of my illness? Did they want to know all the things that made me feel bad? In most cases, no.

They wanted to know that I had hope. They wanted to know that I had the courage to fight my illness. They undoubtedly could tell just by looking at me that I wasn't in the greatest shape—they didn't need me to tell them that. What they needed was reassurance that I believed that I would get well again.

Think about your everyday life. When someone asks you how you are doing, you typically say "fine, great, busy," or something innocuous. I even know people who say "fantastic" in response to the simple question of "How are you doing?" Let's face facts. Most folks don't really care to hear about your problems—they don't expect you to say anything negative.

I realized that I was responding to this simple question in the wrong way during my last illness. When someone would ask me how I was doing, I realized I was pointing out all the things that were still wrong with me. And I wasn't talking at all about the things that were going right. My typical response was, "The left side of my face is still paralyzed; my left eye won't close all the way so it is easily strained; I have a constant headache; and I can't hear out of my left ear."

All of this was true. But, repeatedly talking about it to others, and filling their mind and my mind with these negative thoughts, was not good for anyone.

It didn't take me long to realize I was approaching this all wrong, and I immediately changed my answer to accentuate the positive.

> I am doing better. I have regained some of the muscle tone on the left side of my face. My left eye is closing much better than it did prior to surgery. I can watch some television and read a bit without straining my eyes, and I have found these magical eye drops that help immensely. My headache is manageable. I take just a few extra strength Tylenol each day. So overall, I am steadily improving, and I am confident that I will totally recover in time. It may take me a year, but I *will* recover.

See what a difference accentuating the positive can make? When you look at it, the same facts are presented, but the slant is towards the good things—not the bad. It made me feel better, and it made my friends and family feel better as well.

But, after a few more weeks, I decided that even this was not positive enough. So I changed my answer.

> I'm doing great. The vision in my left eye is no longer blurred or double. I have regained some hearing in my left ear, whereas before surgery I was completely

deaf. My balance has improved dramatically, and I am getting stronger everyday. I am so sure that I will get better that I purchased airline tickets and made hotel reservations for my wife and I to go on a vacation to Yellowstone National Park next month.

Notice the subtle difference. I concentrated on the positives—all the things that have improved and the confidence I have that everything would work out given time.

A corollary to the question "How are you doing?" is, "What happened to you?"

Occasionally I would run into someone that hadn't seen me for a while; just by looking at me they could tell that something major was wrong. After all, my face was droopy, my left eye was sagging and bloodshot, and I could no longer smile. I had to cock my head to the right to hear them.

I could always see it coming. At first they would smile as they recognized me from afar, and yell out "Les." As they approached the expression on their face would change to one of confusion and sometimes horror. They would shake my hand or hug me gently, look at my physical negatives, and then look me square in the eye, and say, "What happened to you?"

At first, this made me very uncomfortable. I really didn't want to rehash what I had been through. I was upset that my appearance made it so obvious that I had had a stroke or some other serious illness. So I would stammer around a little and tell them I had had a brain hemorrhage. The expression on their face would get even grimmer. They were obviously taking pity on me. I didn't need or want their pity.

I was talking with a friend about this one day, and she

recommended humorous first responses when someone looked at me with confusion or horror and asked, "What happened to you?" Here are some of the responses I used:

- "I broke my finger." (Which I did 25 years ago.)
- "Oh, let me show you my better half." (Only the left side of my face was paralyzed, so turning the right side toward them made me appear more normal.)
- "What do you mean? I've always looked funny."

These whimsical answers helped break the ice and lighten the mood. From there I could calmly tell them the real (short) story.

Recently, I met someone for the first time. I have made real progress since the early days and the nerve damage to my face was much less noticeable. Even so, as we shook hands, this person said to me, "Are you okay?" I was having a bad left eye day, and it was a little more droopy and redder than usual. My response was simply, "Of course I'm okay."

So remember the quote at the beginning of this chapter. "A bore is a man who when you ask him how he is, tells you." Most folks really don't want to hear about your problems. A few people very close to you will want to know all the gory details—tell them if they ask. Others will be very empathetic and press you for details—tell them as well. But for the majority of people, a positive, upbeat answer is best for you and them.

Your goal should be to be the happiest, most optimistic sick person possible! It is good for you and also good for the many friends and family who are concerned about you.

And if you look sick, try to lighten the situation with a little humor. Humor is always a good medicine.

BE A NUISANCE

Remember my top ten reasons why it wasn't so bad to have brain surgery in the first chapter? Remember the quip about when a doctor tells you he will take care of something within a week what he really means is, "You may never hear from me again?"

Well, sadly it is sometimes true. The wheels of the medical system move very slowly, and the simplest of things sometimes take way too long to get done. It always seemed especially so for me—patience is not one of my virtues.

It is natural to want things to be done quickly when you are very sick. Why should it take a month to schedule a follow-up MRI? Why should it take six weeks to schedule brain surgery? Why should it take two months to schedule a simple audiogram? All the while, you (I) sit around waiting, stewing about why they don't approach things with the same sense of urgency that we feel. It can be very frustrating!

From my experience, there are a number of reasons why the medical process moves at the pace of a snail. Some of the top reasons are:

- *Medical Insurance Bureaucracy.* Many hospitals and doctors won't do anything (except emergency treatments) without first checking to see if your medical insurance will cover the cost. Conversely, many medical plans require "pre-approval" for medical treatments, which means the insurance company *requires* the doctor to clear treatments and referrals with them prior to taking action. In either case, it takes an army of people and a good deal of time for the doctor's office to consult with your medical insurance company. Meanwhile, the patient waits.

- *Medical System Bureaucracy.* Many hospitals and doctor's offices run on lots of internal paperwork and documentation. Perhaps some of this is to protect themselves from potential malpractice lawsuits. Perhaps much of it is to thoroughly document your condition and treatments, so that other doctors and nurses can quickly come up to speed on what is going on. It is also true that many doctors and hospitals lack modern technical automation, and much of the work is still very manual. Paper and manual processes take more time than those that are automated.

- *Lack of Delegation.* Very little authority is delegated to nurses, nurse's aids, and the others to whom patients have ready access and with whom they have frequent contact. As a hospital patient, I saw a doctor (usually a resident or intern) once a day. I saw my nurse or nurse's aid many times each day. When I asked the nurse for something, invariably he or she had to check with the doctor to get an answer.

As an outpatient, when I called my doctor's office I spoke with an administrative assistant, who took a message for the nurse, who then had to corner the doctor to obtain an answer. Sometimes it would take me two to three days to get a response. As a patient and as someone who has focused on the efficiency of business processes for most of my professional life, I feel that the medical system could benefit from a workflow study and a good dose of delegation of authority

- *Filters.* Although some doctors are better than others, they are all very busy, and many have (deliberately or not) put a variety of "filters" in place that make it difficult for you, the patient, to communicate with them directly. When I called my doctor, I spoke with a medical assistant who took a message. They neither had the information nor the authority to provide answers to questions. The next filter was a nurse, who in many cases could have addressed my question very well, but had to consult with a doctor before giving me an answer. Before my message got to the real doctor, however, the nurse may have consulted with a number of interns or residents. Only after all of this did the doctor get the word. And after going through all these filters, who knows what was communicated and how it was delivered when the doctor finally heard it? All of this took time.

- *Handoffs.* As I've already mentioned, doctors these days are very specialized. The emergency room doctor diagnosed me with Bell's palsy, which was incorrect. He called in neurosurgeons. The first two neurosurgeons were not trained or qualified to perform my surgery—they told me it was too risky. It took three and one-half days to get to someone who was trained and qualified to treat me. My last surgery also required a skull bone specialist, two anesthesiologists, nurses, residents, and a host of other medical staff, all of whose calendars had to be coordinated before a surgery date could be scheduled. Six weeks passed between the time I was diagnosed and the surgery date.

- *Supply and Demand.* Although medical insurance bureaucracy, hospital bureaucracy, filters, and handoffs all slow the process down, the *main* issue, from my perspective, is one of simple supply and demand. We currently do not have enough *exceptional* doctors, nurses, and medical technicians to handle the number of patients requiring care. We don't have enough hospital beds, surgical facilities, and medical equipment to accommodate the increasing demand for medical services. And as baby boomers get older, the problem will potentially worsen.

So what is a patient to do? As with any institution, when the demand for products and services exceeds the supply, the *squeaky wheel* often gets the grease. So being frustrated with the lack of speed at which my problems were being handled, I became an absolute *nuisance*—but a likeable nuisance.

I say likeable nuisance because it wouldn't have helped for me to be regarded as an irritant. I never screamed, hollered, or got upset. Mainly, when things were moving slower than I thought they should, I just made sure they knew I was still around and waiting.

And, I picked my spots. Being a nuisance about everything will also earn you the well-deserved tag of "irritant." For instance, when I was in the hospital, the neurosurgeon told me he would be operating as soon as possible. That was a big relief to me—the sooner the better. I was glad that he was approaching my illness with the same urgency as I felt.

He asked me to call his nurse *immediately* to schedule the surgery. I called her from my hospital bed—and left her a message. After a week of getting no response, I began calling the nurse daily.

When my symptoms began to worsen as I awaited surgery, I called the doctor's office daily until they scheduled me for another CAT scan and a consultation with the doctor. This was important enough to become a really squeaky wheel.

On the other hand, after surgery, my doctor told me I needed an audiogram (hearing test) to evaluate how much of my hearing I had lost, and turned the job of scheduling this over to his assistant. I heard nothing for a month before I called to check the status. Another month went by before I took matters into my own hands and scheduled the appointment by calling someone who accepted my health insurance. There was no need for me to be a pest about an audiogram, since I could schedule that appointment myself.

Here are some ways I found to be squeaky which seemed to work:

- *Go around the filters.* Bypass *all* the filters and take your case directly to the attending physician—that *exceptional* doctor you hired. You can do this in several ways. You can demand that the medical assistant or nurse who answers the phone ask the doctor (not the nurse) to phone you back. If that doesn't work, and the issue is critical, schedule a follow-up appointment with the doctor. Show up in his office for a scheduled appointment, and he will talk with you. Believe me, it will be worth the insurance co-pay. Face-to-face communication is good.

My experience was that when I told the doctor, directly, that I had been waiting weeks for something he had turned over to someone on his staff to schedule, he was not happy; things generally began to move quickly. In fact, on a couple of occasions, just telling the nurse that I wanted to speak with the doctor directly, got things moving. "No need for that," she would say, "I can get that done today." And she did.

- *Threaten to switch to another doctor.* Most doctors are very competitive people—Type A personalities (okay, so am I). And they want your business. In case you haven't noticed, there is a great deal of money at stake. If you have hired an exceptional doctor and you are not satisfied with the speed and urgency with which he and his staff are handling your condition, simply tell the doctor that you are ready to switch to someone else. You may or may not be ready to do that, but just telling the doctor that you are will help. Chances are he will figure out a way to move things along.

- *Put it in writing.* Filters have been highly trained to screen the doctor from patients like you and I, so they may not let you talk to the doctor directly. No worries. Write the doctor a letter and send it to him via fax or registered mail.

After my third brain hemorrhage, my neurosurgeon told me my situation was grave and that no one in Dallas was qualified to treat me. He told me he would refer me to a world-class specialist in another city—and he would do this immediately.

Two weeks went by and I heard nothing. I called his nurse, who explained that much paperwork and documentation (medical bureaucracy) had to be completed before the referral could be made, and that the doctor had not yet completed all of this.

A month later I scheduled a follow-up appointment with the doctor who told me he had simply been too busy (aneurysms, tumors, and other important stuff) to get my referral documentation prepared. Another month went by. In the meantime, I still called his nurse every week to check on the status, and every week his nurse would tell me that the doctor hadn't gotten to it yet.

Understandably frustrated, I prepared a letter reminding him that he had:

- Told me my condition was grave

- Promised to refer me to another doctor quickly

That it had now been two and a half months, and still no referral

The very next day I got a call from the doctor—not the nurse or assistant—saying that my file had been sent, and he expected me to hear something in less than a week. And I did. All I did was put my concerns in writing (*with a copy to my attorney*). Right or wrong, doctors are afraid of written documentation and attorneys.

- *Do your own scheduling.* I waited two months for my neurosurgeon's medical assistant to schedule me for an audiogram. This wasn't urgent and I knew this, but it just seemed as though two months was a bit excessive. I was also interested to know just how much of my hearing had returned, and to find out if a hearing aid could improve my ability to hear. I called the assistant a couple of times and was told he was working on it. I finally picked an ENT clinic at a different facility, and scheduled my own appointment. To this day, four months later, the medical assistant still hasn't called me back.

- *Keep coming back.* After my first brain surgery, my brain was foggy; I found it difficult to concentrate and think. This was a real problem! Believing that something had gone wrong with the surgery, I made numerous follow-ups with my neurosurgeon, each time describing my symptoms. He assured me that what I was experiencing was not normal and that my spacey feelings had nothing to do with my surgery or recovery. In the meantime, I was also seeing my neurologist, describing the same symptoms. Her response was always the same—to increase the dose of my anti-seizure medication. A couple of months went by. First I saw my neurosurgeon who reassured me that I had nothing to worry about. Next I saw my neurologist who increased my medication. Eventually, unbeknownst to me, I was taking twice the recommended maximum dose of anti-seizure medication. And my symptoms were getting worse—not better. It was at this point that my neurosurgeon told me my elevated dosage was causing my problems. "This is what is making you feel spacey," he said. And he recommended a different neurologist who was willing to work with him on my treatments. Listen to your body. If you believe there is something seriously wrong with you, and the doctors can't seem to figure out what it is, be persistent and keep going back.

- *Offer to be a reference.* Sometimes a little bit of sugar goes a long way. After both brain surgeries I wrote my doctor a letter, simply thanking him and his staff for a perfect and flawless surgery, and offering to be a reference should he need one. I think he appreciated this, and although it wasn't my intention, the service I received from his office got even better.

Yes, sometimes waiting for the medical system to get something done is like watching grass grow. And sometimes getting the various departments and people organized for action is like herding cats. This is especially the case when you are a patient with a serious illness. There are many reasons for this, but there are also ways to speed the process up. Whether threatening to change doctors, documenting your questions and concerns in writing, or just scheduling a face-to-face meeting, doctors and their offices can be quite responsive when approached the right way.

AVOID THE BLAME GAME

"Take your life in your own hands and what happens? A terrible thing: no one to blame."

Erica Jong

I had just been diagnosed with my first brain hemorrhage. I was told that my condition was genetic; my immediate reaction was, whose fault is this? Who gave me the bad genes? Was it my mother, my father? Which of my grandparents passed along these bad genes?

Then I was told that, statistically, there is only a 2% chance that a vascular malformation such as mine will bleed. My mind immediately shifted to asking what I had done to beat the odds in the wrong direction.

It must be my fault—something I did. Was it due to my poor eating habits? Had I not taken care of my body? Should I have had more frequent medical check-ups? Should I have lost more weight? Did I work too hard? Maybe I hadn't exercised enough?

If not that, then God must be punishing me for my sins. Why else would an otherwise perfectly healthy forty-two year old man have this problem? I must have done something really bad.

My mind raced from whose genes to blame, to what had I done wrong, to what I had done to be punished. Once I had completed the loop, I revisited all the possibilities again and again.

It reminds me be of that famous Jimmy Buffet song. In the song, the artist laments the fact that he has become a drunken beach bum hooked on margaritas "wasting away again in Margaritaville." Throughout the song he wonders who's to blame for his miserable condition. "Some people claim that there's a woman to blame," but he conjures up other possibilities. His first conclusion is that it's nobody's fault. Upon further reflection he wonders if it might be his own fault. Finally he concludes that it *is* his own fault.

In my case, I have bad genes—three to be exact—that cause vascular malformations in my brain, brain stem, and spine. But many folks live their entire life with these same bad genes, without a single brain hemorrhage. Remember, only 2% of cavernous angiomas bleed. So bad genes are not the only factor.

Could I have taken better care of my body? For my second and third hemorrhages, I was overweight and had high blood pressure. I had failed at scores of diets. But I did exercise regularly. Just prior to my last hemorrhage, I lost fifty pounds in twelve months; I was walking three to six miles a day, and my resting pulse was fifty. I was in great shape. But this didn't keep me from having a hemorrhage. So taking better care of my body wasn't the answer.

So was it God's fault? Most certainly not. The God I believe in is a loving God. He is our heavenly father, and like our earthly father, he suffers when his children suffer. I don't believe that God would intentionally inflict a serious illness on me, or any one of his earthly children.

Still it is human nature to search for an answer the questions of whom or what is to blame. Sometimes it is good to pinpoint the cause. If a person knows what caused their illness, they can take action to avoid the same thing happening again. If you have had a heart attack, for instance, you may find out it happened because your arteries were clogged. Knowing this, your doctor can place stints in your vessels, so the blood can flow more freely. Subsequently, you can exercise more, take medications, and change your diet to prevent a recurrence.

In my case, the root cause of a brain hemorrhage is a little more elusive. Certainly high blood pressure is a factor. And high blood pressure intensified by high stress situations or strenuous activity should be avoided. I must also avoid foods and medications that thin my blood. Thicker blood and lower stress will minimize the risks of further bleeds.

Knowing this is certainly helpful, but the bottom line is that there is no one to blame for my condition. Jimmy Buffet had it right the first time. The fact is that it is nobody's fault. Stuff happens. And, yes, sometimes bad stuff happens to good people. Further, it is counterproductive to spend time and energy trying to identify the culprit.

Unfortunately we live in a society where someone or something needs to be blamed when bad things happen. Take Hurricane Katrina. This was a tragic disaster and God bless all those who lost their lives, their homes, their city—they lost everything. But this rush to blame the city, state, federal, and local government for not being responsive—someone needed to remind the world that this was the worst natural disaster in our country's history. In the aftermath of Hurricane Katrina, government officials are making it clear that they cannot respond to a catastrophe of this magnitude, should one happen again in the future. It's just not possible.

My other favorite example of our society's blame game is road rage. Road rage happens when the driver of a car gets angry about what someone else has done on the road. Usually the driver has been cut off in traffic or another driver has failed to let him merge into a line of traffic— something minute like that. In short the driver becomes enraged. The answer is that all drivers need to control their tempers when they are behind the wheel of what can be a deadly weapon.

But our society has decided that this is not the angry driver's fault after all. Instead, it is caused by something called Intermittent Explosive Disorder (IED). As I understand it, IED transforms a simple bad temper to "temporary insanity" on the road. It is a medical condition that should be treated—not something human beings can be held responsible for. Rubbish!

So whether it be human nature or our culture, it seems we are inclined to seek blame. Patients often beat themselves up trying to affix blame for their illness. Is it my fault? Is it my parent's fault? Is it God's fault? When in fact, it's nobody's fault, and it is a waste of time and energy to engage in such a witch-hunt. Sometimes stuff just happens.

NO STINKIN' THINKIN'

"Never lose your trust. Do not be defeated. Do not be discouraged. Do not cut yourselves off from the roots from which we have our origins"

Pope John Paul II

The first step in getting well is *to know* that you *will* get better. The definition of faith is not that you *believe* God *can* do something, but rather that you *know* he *will* do it. You may understandably begin by wondering whether you will ever get better. If your faith is strong, however, you will quickly understand that you only need place your fate in God's hands.

I visit the sick in the hospital on a regular basis. One day I met two men—both of whom had just had hip replacements. While talking with the first man, I asked him how long he expected his recovery to last. His response was, "I expect to be up and around in a couple of months." When I asked the same question of the second man, his response was, "I am in so much pain now. I'll never be able to walk normal again." The man with the "I'm going to be up and around in no time" attitude made a much better recovery that the man with the "I may never walk normal again" attitude. They had identical surgeries and were the same age; they were even in the same good health. The only difference between them was their attitude.

One of the best ways to improve your physical health is to make sure that your mental health and spiritual health are strong. One of the most important things you can do to improve your mental health and strengthen your spiritual life is to find a way to fill your mind with uplifting thoughts.

Your thoughts filter down to your emotions. Happy thoughts will lift you from the doldrums. Poisonous thoughts will make you feel sad. Much emotional pain is the direct result of "stinkin' thinkin'"—poisonous thoughts!

I realize it is hard to think positively when you feel horrible. So how did I do it? I started by counting my blessings and by filling my mind with uplifting thoughts. I focused on the positive—no matter how bad things may have seemed, I always found something to be grateful for. I discovered that I had the power to change the bad habit of being down in the dumps. The mind only has room for one set of thoughts at a time. When I thought good thoughts, the toxic ones didn't have room to fester.

Here's the trick. Do not identify with your thoughts. Instead of being your thoughts, be the observer of your thoughts. When you observe yourself slipping into a negative state of mind, stop and distance yourself from thoughts that upset you. Stay focused on those things that bring you joy.

For instance, when I was at my lowest point, my mind

would sometimes drift toward the negative—such as the fact that I couldn't close my left eye to shower, the fact that I drooled when I ate and drank, the fact that I had no energy, the fact that I had a constant headache, and so on and so on. Would I ever get better? Would my brain ever function properly again? What would my end-state be? Would I be able to work again? Would anyone even hire me?

As soon as I caught my mind dwelling on these negatives, I deliberately changed my thoughts to all the positives in my life. I took an inventory of the things I was grateful for. For instance:

- I am alive
- My condition is not terminal
- I can feed myself and swallow
- My arms and legs are not paralyzed
- I have no complications or collateral damage as a result of surgery
- My mind is still sharp
- I am improving every week
- One of my doctors and all of my therapists make house calls
- The company I work for is taking very good care of me
- A lot of people are praying for me
- I have a great wife
- I have three wonderful sons and one fantastic daughter-in-law

- I will live to see my grandchildren
- I *will* make a full recovery

And there were many additional things I had to be grateful for, but the point is that there were a lot of positives to override the negatives. I wrote these down on a piece of paper and every time my mind would drift toward negative thoughts, I'd pull it out and remind myself that there were so many more positives to think about.

Turn to nature to break the spell of despair and despondency. I love to watch birds. After my first brain surgery, we placed extra bird feeds in our yard so I had a vantage point to watch the birds feed from almost any window. I found a tranquil lake surrounded by beautiful trees, quiet walking trails and ornate rock formations about an hour from my home, and my wife and I would spend hours there almost every week. It can be done—not easily perhaps, but with determination you can find peace.

Turn to the Lord, and ask for help. Poisonous thoughts will hang around only as long as you do nothing to dispel them. Instead of wallowing in the past or worrying about the future, let your eyes, ears, nose, taste buds, and sense of touch lead you to a new plateau of enjoyment.

Three examples of stinkin' thinkin' are as follows:

1. The fear of failure: What if I don't recover? What if I can't whip this thing?

2. The fear of danger: What if I get worse? What if the doctor didn't get it all out? What if I have another brain hemorrhage?

3. The fear of facing life squarely: This is too much for

me to bear. I don't have the strength to battle my way back. I just wish that I were dead."

Notice that all three involve fear. Fear is a poisonous intruder. Banish these fears as you would a bunch of mice running around in your living room. Otherwise they will destroy your life.

You are not your thoughts. They don't own you. You are the observer of your thoughts, and you can wish away the ones that are not from God. Substitute uplifting thoughts for poisonous ones. Cultivate a more positive attitude through mental discipline and prayer.

St. Theresa of Avila used to repeat the following mantra to herself over and over: "Let nothing disturb you; let nothing cause you fear. God is unchanging love. He will protect you."

MAKE RECOVERY
YOUR FULL TIME JOB

"The only thing that overcomes hard luck is hard work."

Harry Golden

U.S. journalist (1902–1981)

My first thoughts after all my illnesses were about getting better. I had instantly lost my ability to see, hear, chew food, walk, work, drive—these and so many other things that I had previously taken for granted. They were all gone, and I wanted them back more than anything else in the world!

On the other hand, I never considered that my nerve damage would be permanent. I just didn't let my mind go there. I was immediately focused on getting well. I was determined to get back the physical strength and stamina that the trauma of brain surgery had drained from me.

My doctors would often examine me; they would tell me that I had suffered severe nerve damage and that I was unlikely to fully recover. I would look back at them—straight into their eyes—and tell them that I planned to recover 100%. They, in turn, would look at me as though

I was from another planet. Like I was insane. One of my doctors even called me cocky. I enjoyed that!

So I made recovery my full-time job. After all, I had nothing else to do. Once a hemorrhage occurred and even more so after brain surgery, I was unable to do my normal job. The only way I could resume normal activities was to recover. The only way I could continue to live a normal life was to recover. In my mind, I had no other option.

Occasionally a friend or acquaintance would say to me, "*If* you get better...." I would quickly interrupt them and say, "You mean *when* I get better. Because I will get better!"

Recovery was not only my full-time job, it was the hardest job I've ever done—and I've done some pretty hard jobs. It also took more courage than anything else I've ever done. The harder I worked, the more complete and quicker my recoveries were. Imagine that!

The sooner I started the better. Twenty-four hours after my first brain surgery, I was up and out of my ICU hospital bed. I shed my hospital gown for my own pajamas and was demanding the nurse order me a full, cooked breakfast. I hadn't eaten solid food in nearly forty-eight hours, so I was starving.

I tried to get out of bed on my own, just twenty-four hours after my second surgery, but I failed miserably. I just couldn't stand up and put one foot in front of the other. The surgery had been far more traumatic, and I was fifty-seven years old—not forty-three years old this time.

Fortunately I had a lot of help with my recovery. Two days later, a nice occupational therapist stopped by my hospital room to teach me how to get around with a walker. I managed to get out of my room and walked down the hall two doors away, although I decided right away that this walker thing definitely had to go. The occupational therapist also taught me how to get in and out of a shower, even though I lacked complete mobility. She taught me how to climb a few stairs with my walker—both upstairs and downstairs.

Another two days went by. A speech therapist came by to watch me eat and swallow to make sure things were working okay. She didn't like what she saw, so she ordered a barium x-ray of my head and throat.

This was an interesting test. I sat in a chair and a real-time x-ray machine was directed at my head and throat. The speech therapist mixed barium into a variety of foods and drinks, each with a different consistency. Then I ate the foods while the therapist, my wife, and I watched the skeleton of my head chew and then swallow. Right there on the x-ray you could see the barium-enriched food going down the skeletal throat. Amazing! My wife says it was funny to watch a skeleton eat. What we learned was that I couldn't swallow dense foods on the first try, but that a second try did the trick. Good news.

After I was discharged from the hospital, my doctor ordered in-home physical and speech therapy. I was officially declared *homebound*, which meant that I lacked the strength and stamina to get into a car and have my wife drive me for treatments outside my house.

My physical therapist, Peter, was very good. His job was to help me get my strength, stamina, and balance back. He came to my house three times a week for six weeks. He taught me how to do low impact sit-ups on the couch. He taught me how to do squats from a sitting position on a chair. He followed me around the house and watched me walk (at first in a walker, and then two weeks later a few steps on my own). He taught me some balance exercises to help restore my equilibrium and keep me from falling. He increased the difficulty level of these and other exercises as my strength and stamina improved.

During his visits he observed me doing the exercises he had prescribed. He would then leave and tell me to repeat them all at least twice each day. I did exactly what he asked.

After six weeks, my well-being and endurance had improved, I was no longer homebound, and I had learned all the right exercises. I had dispensed with the walker, although I still had some residual balance issues. Peter quit coming to the house, and I continued to exercise on my own until I was able to walk outside.

Walking outside was a real challenge for me. I was still a bit wobbly from the hemorrhage and surgery. To make it more challenging, I had a very steep driveway. I just couldn't get from my front door to the sidewalk—*if only I could get to that sidewalk!*. So I walked laps around the ground floor of my home for several weeks. When I was finally able to negotiate the steep driveway, I began walking outdoors. Something I still do today.

I also had help from Lisa, an in-home speech therapist. Two weeks after I was released from the hospital, she started coming by to see me. She also came three times a week. Her main job was to help restore the paralyzed muscles on the left side of my face, which made my face droopy—and made it difficult for me to speak and eat. She did this with electrical stimulation.

It was quite funny, actually. It reminded me of scenes in the movies where someone is being tortured with electrical shocks. It hurt, but the pain was nothing compared to my desire to get back to normal.

She came armed with a little machine that produced electrical current. She hooked electrodes to the left side of my face. There was a dial on the machine to turn up the juice. Fortunately, she would turn control of the dial over to me, so at least it was self-torture. I would crank up the current until I couldn't stand it anymore. The electrodes sent a constant electric shock to my facial nerves in an attempt to wake them up and get them functioning again. We did this for forty-five minutes, three times a week.

Lisa also taught me some facial exercises to help regain my muscle strength. She told me it was her goal to make me look as ridiculous as she possibly could, stretching and making faces that worked my facial muscles. She succeeded— I looked pretty silly. When she wasn't around, I practiced these exercises religiously, several times a day.

My in-home speech therapist administered electrical nerve stimulation for about a month, after which I continued for another month on an outpatient basis.

I also pursued some non-traditional treatments with the consent of my doctor. For instance, Peter, my physical therapist recommended a different type of electrical stimulation—one that sent pulses of electric shocks to the nerves rather than a constant stream of electrical current. He helped me locate a machine from a medical supply house, and he trained my wife on how and where to administer the shock. My medical insurance didn't cover the cost, but I was determined to do whatever it took to get well.

My wife "shocked" my face several times a week for six months. I joked that she seemed to enjoy this electric shock treatment far too much.

I also pursued acupuncture to help restore my facial muscle function. In one week, three different friends independently asked me if I had considered acupuncture. One friend asked me on Monday, another on Wednesday, and a third friend on Friday. After the third person asked, I got the hint. Maybe acupuncture was something I needed to try.

I hadn't even considered it, but three people mentioning it in one week was too much of a coincidence to ignore. I got on the Internet and did some research. It turned out that acupuncture has proven to be quite successful in reversing facial paralysis. I went for treatments twice a week—one hour each time—for three months. I think it helped me immensely. Again, my medical insurance didn't cover this expense. At first this bothered me, until a good friend said, "You're health is worth it."

I also invented some of my own therapies. I recognized, early on, that regaining the vision in my left eye was the most critical challenge I faced. Frankly, I was getting no medical advice on how to accomplish this. So I reasoned it out. I had a lot of pain in my left eye, a burning, irritating sort of pain. Using my left eye to read or watch TV made the pain unbearable.

But I forged through the irritation and pain and forced myself to use it. The vision in my left eye was one of the first things to come back!

All of this was very hard work. It was literally a full time job. At the peak of my rehabilitation I was doing:

- In-home physical exercises with my physical therapist, three times a week for an hour each time.

- Additional physical exercises on my own, seven days a week, one hour each time.

- Forty-five minutes of electrical stimulation administered by my speech therapist, three times a week.

- Acupuncture twice a week, one hour each time.

- Multiple laps around the house every day for thirty minutes.

- Electric shock treatments given by my wife, twice daily.

- Watching television with my left eye an hour each day

- Reading a book with my left eye an hour each day

And, I was doing all of this when I felt just dreadful. When you tack on travel time, I was a pretty busy guy. Not to mention physically exhausted.

I have gotten to know many brain trauma patients in recent years. I can tell you that those who don't work hard—those who don't pursue every possible opportunity to regain their neurological skills—just don't get better.

Physical, speech, and occupational therapists are wonderful human beings. I was fortunate to have some of the best. My advice is to use them. Take advantage of all the recovery tools your medical insurance will provide. And when your medical insurance doesn't cover a treatment you require, take the advice of my good friend and do it anyway—you're worth it.

The key to all of this therapy is to start small and ramp up as you are able. The second key is to do *exactly* what they tell you to do.

My path to recovery included physical therapy, speech

therapy, occupational therapy, acupuncture, and a host of other activities. Make recovery your full-time job and devote all your energy and attention to the task at hand. It may be the hardest job you've ever done.

When I returned to my neurosurgeon—three months after surgery—I had made huge progress. He (the same guy who had told me I would not fully recover and had also told me that I was cocky) was amazed. At the time, my left eye was still droopy. When I asked him about surgery, his response was, "No, let's give it more time. Given the progress you've made so far, it will probably come back on its own." This was music to my ears!

PACE YOURSELF

"The elevator to success is out of order. You'll have to use the stairs...one step at a time."

Joe Girard

I recently visited a friend who had undergone brain surgery to remove a brain aneurysm. I visited her in the hospital three times, and all three times she was sound asleep—a deep, soothing, peaceful sleep.

I'm just not made that way. As soon as I come down with even the slightest cold or flu, my tendency is to try to be up and around, doing something—anything. The sicker I get the more determined I become to get well. So after each brain hemorrhage or brain surgery, I was really determined to get well.

Sometimes I wish I were more like my friend. She was relaxed and calm following one of the most traumatic events of her life. I, on the other hand, am usually anxious and eager to do whatever I can to *not* be sick.

I think the initial stages of recovery are best spent resting, sleeping, and letting the body heal. However in my case, once this initial period of rest was over, I was better off trying to get up and around as soon as possible. The longer

I lay dormant, the weaker my body got. With each of my illnesses, I had two short-term goals:

1. To be up and around as quickly as possible.
2. To be able to do things on my own—without assistance—as soon as possible.

In my case, my body was severely weakened from the trauma of a brain hemorrhage. Then weakened even more by brain surgery. And finally weakened by the long periods of immobility that accompanied them both. I needed to regain both my muscle tone and endurance following these separate but related events.

In addition, I suffered nerve damage from each brain hemorrhage. Nerve damage heals slowly. I learned that I couldn't just go from being bed-bound and unable to walk to running around the block overnight. I learned that recovery comes in baby steps. In short, I learned to pace myself.

At first, it was hard for me to understand why surgery made me feel much, much worse instead of making me feel better. I expected the just the opposite. I expected that surgery would *fix* me up and improve my health. I learned that both the hemorrhages and the surgeries are major traumas to the body—independent traumas that require healing and recovery.

Brain surgery doesn't heal nerve damage. It only keeps the damage from getting worse. If I had not had surgery to remove the problematic veins in my brain, they would have continued to bleed, and I would have suffered even more nerve damage. My neurological condition would have gradually worsened.

With surgery, the bleeding (and a source of future bleeding) was removed, and I was given an opportunity to let my body's natural healing abilities go to work. But make no mistake about it—surgery will make you feel much worse, temporarily, before you begin to feel better.

I suffered my last hemorrhage at a point when I was in fairly good physical shape. I had lost fifty pounds in the previous twelve months and was walking three to six miles a day. My resting pulse was in the high forties or low fifties. I was fifty-seven years old, and it was a good thing I was in such great shape. It made my recovery easier.

No matter how much I wanted to get back in the swing of things in weeks—not months—it took me months to recover. Recovery is a gradual process. I recovered one step at a time, and I was grateful for every step forward I took along the way.

Following all my illnesses, the very first activity I resumed was going to church. My faith is very important to me, and I missed being able to attend church services when I was in the hospital and later when I was homebound. For my first brain surgery, they shaved my head. And the incision was long and ugly. I definitely stood out in a crowd with my shaved head and a big gash in my skull. I was self-conscious about my appearance. At the time, my sons were all teenagers and I remember asking them, "Will you be embarrassed to go to church with me?" They said, "No way." That was a godsend.

I didn't just come home from the hospital and start attending church services. I worked my way back, one step at a time. The first step was sitting in a chair and watching Mass on the Eternal Word Television Network, the Catholic television network founded by Mother Angelica. As soon as I was able, I attended a daily mass at my local church. Daily masses at my church last about thirty minutes and have between twenty-five to thirty-five people in attendance. This was all I could handle for awhile.

As my strength and balance improved, I went to a Sunday Mass. Sunday Mass lasts about an hour and has 400–500 people in attendance. At first this was difficult for me, because I was still wobbly and didn't do well navigating my way through crowds; I just came early and left late to avoid the rush. It took me four months to be able to attend a church service in a normal fashion. I did it one step at a time. I paced myself.

The same goes for walking. This is something most of us take for granted. Not me. It took me months to regain the balance and strength I needed to walk normally, and it took me ten months to get back to my pre-surgery condition.

My first steps following surgery were with a walker. When I came home from the hospital, it was a real struggle to make it up the three small steps from my driveway to the front door of my home. Boy, did that motivate me to get rid of that walker!

My first steps without a walker were the four steps I took from my recliner to the kitchen table. These were four challenging steps. I took them slowly and with great concentration to make sure that I didn't lose my balance and fall down. And, these first steps on my own were made under my wife's careful watchful eye. Occasionally I'd have to grab onto her to keep my balance.

I gradually worked up to walking ten laps around the house—then fifteen laps around the house, and eventually all the way up to thirty laps around the house. I celebrated each and every milestone along the way.

I was really excited when I was strong enough to walk

outside. Walking around the house was pretty boring. It wasn't very scenic. There was no fresh breeze blowing in my face, no sun shining on my body, and no birds singing. Walking outside in the fresh spring air was much better. I was only able to walk up and down the street a few houses. Then my strength got better and I walked half a block. By June (four months after surgery), I was walking one to two miles a day; by July I was walking three miles a day. I wasn't walking as fast or with the confidence I had prior to surgery, but I was walking.

I had worked my way from four difficult steps from the recliner to the kitchen table all the way up to three miles outside in five months time. I did it by gradually building up my strength and stamina—by pacing myself.

I love to play golf. I'm somewhat addicted. But, golf was on the low end of the priority scale after my last episode. In fact, there was a brief period when I wasn't sure I would ever play golf again, and frankly I didn't care. I had much bigger issues to overcome—such as seeing, hearing, walking, and driving again.

One day a friend of mine asked me if I was playing any golf yet. I said no. He said, "Well, are you at least putting?" I said no—not yet. His response was, "You ought to at least be putting. You could do that on the carpet inside your house." He was right.

So my first step back toward playing golf was putting on the carpet inside my house. My next step was chipping in my backyard. I live on a golf course, so my next step was walking out my back gate, onto the course, and hitting five balls out into the fairway. I hit those same five balls back toward my house (Don't worry, I'm pretty good, and no one's windows were at risk!).

I remember my first thought. *Wow! I can still hit a golf ball.* Seeing it after I hit it was a bit challenging, but I struck the ball clean, and it went straight. This was about three months after surgery.

I continued to practice putting, chipping, and hitting balls out onto the fairway. Two weeks later I went to the driving range and hit fifty balls. The next week I hit 100 balls. The following week I played nine holes—riding in a power cart. This was about four months after surgery. By June, I was playing eighteen holes once a week. And by July I was playing eighteen holes twice a week—with my great golfing buddies.

These guys helped me a lot at first. They drove me around, helped me watch and find my ball, did the bending over to take the ball out of the hole and repair ball marks, and tons of other things which enabled me—a handicapped person—to enjoy one of my favorite activities. I wore down a bit with about six holes to go, but I did finish all eighteen holes. Afterward, I drove home and went to bed.

Driving a vehicle is a key activity for those of us who are disabled. By driving I got my independence back—I could go wherever I wanted to go when I wanted to go there. My brain hemorrhages left me with dizziness and a spacey feeling—like I wasn't all there. I felt brain damaged. After my last hemorrhage, I also had vision problems. Driving under these conditions was out of the question. My wife was my chauffeur for several months.

It took about three and a half months for my dizziness and spacey feelings to subside. My vision came back sooner. Once I felt able to drive, I started by driving around the block in our neighborhood. The next step was driving short distances, such as the mile from my home to the grocery store. Eventually, I graduated to driving a few miles to my doctor's office. All of this was done on back roads and city streets—no freeways—under my wife's watchful eye.

At about the five-month mark, I was able to drive on freeways again. At first my wife accompanied me, but today (nine months after surgery) I am driving pretty much normal—and by myself!

There were some things I couldn't control or do anything about. Both brain hemorrhages and brain surgeries caused me to have headaches. I mean terrible headaches. Following my third hemorrhage, I had migraine level headaches for thirteen months. I took a mild migraine headache medication throughout this period until—one day—the headaches just went away. The headaches that followed my most recent hemorrhage and surgery were not nearly as bad. I take extra strength Tylenol daily to keep them in check. There was no pacing myself with headaches and other physical healing—just patiently waiting it out until the body healed.

If you are anything like me, you will not only want to get well, but you will want to do it fast. But here is the bottom line. With all my brain hemorrhages, it took an entire year (give or take a month or two) to get *fully* back to normal. No matter how severe or light the nerve damage was, no matter how weakened I was, no matter how good or bad my physical condition was before the hemorrhage or surgery, it took a year to get it all back. Many things came back sooner, but it was a full year before *everything* healed. Just in case I haven't mentioned it, nerve damage heals slowly.

As I sit in my home office today, nine months after my last surgery, I am physically strong and able, but still have neurological damage that is healing.

My recovery has been a slow process. It has definitely been a marathon, not a sprint. I paced myself and wasn't disappointed when I wasn't able to do everything the way I used to for a few weeks or months. I approached every activity as I did walking, playing golf, and driving. I started out small and pushed myself to go a little more each week. I listened to my body, and it told me what I was capable of doing and what needed to wait.

And, when I tried to do too much, too soon, my body let me know right away. So now, let's talk about setbacks.

SETBACKS

"Life is a series of experiences, each one of which makes us bigger, even though it is hard to realize this. For the world was built to develop character, and we must learn that the setbacks and grief which we endure help us in our marching onward."

Unknown

I always felt emotionally better once surgery was over. Then, and only then, did I know for sure that I could still speak, eat, walk, swallow, etc. by myself. It was always nice to confirm that I wouldn't be spending the rest of my life in a wheelchair or with someone else caring for me.

With brain surgery, there is a chance that the surgeons can damage other nerves in the process of removing a tumor or, in my case, my twisted bleeding veins. So I was always relieved to find out that I was still functional, and that I could begin to work to return to a normal life.

But not before I put in a lot of hard work recovering and rehabilitating. I made recovery my full time job. I worked hard at it. I pushed myself as hard as I could in order to get better as soon as possible.

Sometimes I was too driven and paid the price with a setback. I remember the first time I tried to go from walking ten laps around the house to walking twenty-five laps around the house. My body quickly let me know that I wasn't ready for twenty-five laps. I was exhausted, and it took me days to bounce back to my ten lap walks.

Then there was the infamous nosebleed incident. In that interim period between being diagnosed with a brain hemorrhage and having surgery to fix the problem, I needed to have a follow-up MRI to confirm that the bleeding had stopped and that swelling in the brain had been reduced. My wife drove me to the hospital where I needed a wheelchair to get from the car to the MRI facility. Once there I underwent a series of MRIs that lasted for more than one hour. I waited another thirty minutes to get the films so I could take them to my doctor. My wife then wheeled me up to the doctor's office, where I waited another ninety minutes to see the doctor (to be fair, he was working me in, and I knew that I would have to wait in advance). The doctor gave me a favorable report. I went home exhausted.

I had already broken all sorts of records. I had been out of the house, ridden in a car, and gone up and down elevators in a hospital for nearly six hours. This was the most activity I had had since before my brain hemorrhage. All I wanted to do was go to bed.

So I went to bed, for fifteen seconds—literally. As soon as my head hit the pillow, my nose began to bleed profusely. It was gushing blood. Nothing I did slowed the bleeding, so my wife took me back to the emergency room.

I pinched my nose until the emergency room crew arrived to try to stop the bleeding by packing my nose. Now, if you've never had your nose packed, let me just tell you that you don't want to. It hurts. And in my case, packing my nose did not stop the bleeding. Blood-soaked towels were everywhere—not to mention my now bloody shirt. Better to have a bleeding nose than to have a bleeding brain, I kept telling myself. But I was exhausted!

Repetitive nose packing wasn't working. I finally suggested that the nurse allow me to go back to pinching my nose, and she agreed. So I sat in a bed in the emergency room for another two and a half hours waiting for an ear, nose, and throat doctor to arrive. All the while I was pinching my nose.

When the ear, nose, and throat doctor came, he instructed me to continue pinching my nose while he laid out all the grim options—most of which involved surgery. Eventually, he instructed me to quit pinching my nose and, praise the Lord, the bleeding had stopped!

He agreed to let me go home. My day ended, having spent six hours in the hospital for MRIs and a doctor's consultation, and then another four hours in the emergency room nursing a bloody nose. This turned out to be a ten-hour day for me—someone who had just three weeks earlier suffered a serious brain hemorrhage. It took me a full week to bounce back from this.

After my first brain surgery, the doctor told me it would be three to six months before I could return to work. I heard the three-month part, but somehow missed the six-month comment. So I tried to go back to my office job in three months. I lasted three days before I was back home recovering. Another month went by—me sitting at home trying to take it easy, while at the same time trying to build back my endurance.

At the four month point I went back to work. I failed

again. This time I lasted five days. I returned to my "recovery work" at home and didn't attempt another return until I was sure I was good and ready!

I suffered many setbacks along the way. At first, when my body was still weak and I lacked both strength and stamina, a setback would last a week. It was frustrating that it took a full week just to get back to where I had been before I had pushed myself too hard. As I became stronger, my setbacks lasted only a day. And, eventually, I could recover from a setback with a short nap or by sitting quietly in a comfortable chair.

You will probably suffer setbacks as well, especially if you are as driven to get well as I was. How will you know it? Your body will tell you. Remember to listen to your body. In fact sometimes your body will punish you for trying to do too much too soon.

But don't confuse setbacks with relapses. My setbacks caused me to slow it down and take it easier. A relapse would have landed me back in the hospital. Let me tell you about a relapse involving a friend of mine.

She had a large tumor removed from the left frontal lobe of her brain. The surgery went well, her neurological functions were good, and she was released from the hospital to recover and rehabilitate at home. Everything was going well.

One week later, she noticed a sudden decline in her neurological health. Her headaches increased severely, her balance got much worse, and she lost her short-term memory. She was rushed back to the hospital where she was diagnosed with fluid and swelling on the brain. The doctor drilled a hole in her skull to drain the fluid and placed her on anti-inflammatory steroids to reduce the swelling (common treatments for brain injuries). Two weeks later she was back home again, resting and recovering.

And then there are micro-bleeds. Like most people with my condition, I just don't have one malformed vein in my brain, brainstem, and spine, I have many. Once a malformed vein is surgically removed, it won't bleed anymore; however, it is possible that some of these others will bleed. Oftentimes, the bleeding is slight. Neurosurgeons call these micro-bleeds. Even micro-bleeds can cause minor neurological problems, but the damage is usually minor and short-lived. They don't require treatment, and they won't land you in the hospital.

My neurosurgeon showed me my MRI and pointed to all the cavernous angiomas that were in my brain, brainstem, and spine. I could see them clearly. One of the reasons they were so clear is that almost all of them had bled just a little and small traces of dried blood surrounded each vascular malformation. "Micro-bleeds are very common with your condition," the doctor said. "All of these cavernomas will bleed just a little from time to time. You may not notice them, or you may experience a temporary headache, some minor dizziness, or small balance issues. Unless there is significant neurological damage (loss of speech, memory loss, disorientation, numbness, severe weakness, etc.), they are nothing to worry about." Easy for him to say!

So how can you and I tell the difference between a setback, a micro-bleed, and a relapse? A setback will make you feel overly tired, and drain your strength. A micro-bleed may present some minor neurological symptoms. Relapses, on the other hand, are marked with a sudden and severe change in neurological health. With my friend, the key was her sudden loss of short-term memory. And relapses will land you back in the hospital.

THE VIRTUE OF PATIENCE

"A handful of patience is worth more than a bushel of brains"

Dutch Proverb

It's a fact. Patience is not one of my virtues. Just ask my wife. In the words of Larry the Cable Guy, I am a "git er done" kind of guy.

When it came to getting the care I deserved in a timely manner, I could easily become a real nuisance. But once the treatment had been administered, and I was in the recovery stage of my illness, I learned to become much more patient.

I learned that the body requires time to heal. I learned that nerve damage takes a *very* long time to heal. Waiting for damaged nerves to heal gave new meaning to the phrase "time is the ultimate healer." Without patience I would have gone nuts.

Take a look at the definition of the word patience.

1. "The state or quality of being patient; the power of suffering with fortitude; uncomplaining endurance of evils or wrongs, as toil, pain, poverty, insult, oppression, calamity, etc.

2. The act or power of calmly or contentedly waiting for something due or hoped for; forbearance."[4]

These definitions hit the nail on the head. They talk about suffering with fortitude and uncomplaining endurance of evils or wrongs. I did this a lot when I was sick. And they talk about the act of calmly or contentedly waiting for something due or hoped for. Amen, brother!

Was I always tolerant? The answer is no. I wanted badly to get well and I wanted it *now*—not six to twelve months from now.

With my first two brain hemorrhages, I lacked patience and felt real fear. I wasted valuable energy worrying about how slow my recovery was moving. I stopped some of my post-surgery therapy and treatments because I wasn't seeing immediate results. I wasn't counting my blessings, and I ignored the positive gains I had made on the road to recovery. And I felt irritated, agitated, ignored, frustrated, resentful, and anxious.

Hindsight is 20–20. I realized after I recovered from my first two hemorrhages that fear and anxiety had hurt me even more. I suffered from the trauma of a brain hemorrhage, and then I suffered again by not being patient with what, by definition, would be a long recovery. I realized that I didn't want to experience those feelings again.

Fortunately I have mellowed. In spite of all the frustrations surrounding a serious illness I gradually learned to become more patient. I did this by:

- *Visualizing my desired outcome.* A friend of mine once told me that many victims of the Holocaust survived by visualizing that they would be set free, and further visualizing what they would do when they were free—reuniting with family, going back to their jobs, vacationing on the French Riviera. Throughout their captivity, they focused on their individual desired outcome.

Likewise, many professional athletes visualize a desired outcome as part of their mental game. Some of the world's best golfers visualize hitting the perfect shot, with a little right to left draw, directly into the middle of the fairway just prior to swinging their club.

My desired outcome was to recover fully from my hemorrhage and then dedicate my life to teaching others how to achieve the same result. This is what I visualized and what I kept my mind focused on.

- *Letting go of my need for instant gratification.* We live in a society of instant gratification. When we want something we take out a credit card and buy it. We even have instant messaging (IM) and text messaging—email apparently isn't fast enough.

I learned that healing takes time. I learned to celebrate the smallest steps forward; these interim milestones became my instant gratifications. For instance, I celebrated and rejoiced the day some of my hearing came back. I celebrated and rejoiced the first day I opened my left eye and could see again. I celebrated the first day I was able to walk without a walker. And I told myself that there were more of these improvements to come, given time. I learned to break down my larger goal of making a full recovery into manageable chunks and to be grateful for achieving these milestones along the way to full recovery.

- *Taking things one day at a time*. It may be a cliché, but taking things one day at a time is a good way to keep calm while surviving a serious illness. I treated each day of life as a gift from God that allowed me to get one step closer to my goal of full recovery. I worked hard to remember that the future comes one day at a time.

- *Knowing that I had done everything possible to achieve my desired outcome*. I had hired the very best doctors available. I was undergoing physical, occupational, and speech therapy. I was paying for acupuncture treatments twice a week. I was avoiding strenuous activity and keeping my blood pressure down. I came to realize that I was doing everything that I could do to get better.

- *Letting Go and Letting God*. Another good friend of mine taught me this simple mantra. For some reason, I think I'm in control of my life. I like to decide what I need most, what I will do next, what I want to accomplish, and how others will think of me. I am so busy running my own life, I hardly have time for anything else.

And yet thinking back over the past twenty years, there is no way I would have imagined ending up where I am now. So I realize that I am *not* in control of my life. I especially recognized that my physical condition is not in my control, and I let go and turned the outcome over to God.

- *Finding peace in my suffering.* I worked to feel peace, contentment, and satisfaction, believing I was on the path to recovery. Prayer helped me a lot with this. My prayers and the prayers others said on my behalf.

- *Making fear my enemy.* Was I afraid when my brain bled? Yes. Was I anxious when I learned that I needed brain surgery? Of course. The first thing I did was to give myself permission to be afraid— after all I had a serious illness.

But I made my fear a temporary condition by realizing that being afraid was offensive to God; after all it meant I didn't trust him with the outcome. I gradually learned that fear was my worst enemy. It kept me from being positive. It kept me from visualizing my end-state of full recovery. So I made up my mind that fear would not be a part of me.

So work on your patience. Learn to let go and let God. Take life a little easier—one day at a time. And treat everyday as a gift. Don't worry about what happened yesterday and don't anticipate what might happen tomorrow. Focus on your goal of a full recovery, and then break that goal down into manageable steps. Be grateful and celebrate the small steps you take forward—and I mean really celebrate!

IT'S ONLY TEMPORARY

"Please stand by we are experiencing temporary technical difficulties normal programming
will return shortly."
A message from your local television network

I had just suffered my first brain hemorrhage. I was weak, nauseous, disoriented, and too dizzy to stand up let alone walk. The left side of my body was numb and weak. I was unable to dress myself; I had to crawl to the bathroom; and I couldn't walk without holding onto something, let alone drive or work. I was in bad shape. Just one year later I was back to normal—fully recovered.

I had my first brain surgery in February 1992. My head hurt like no pain I had ever experienced. My body was trau-matized by the huge incision in my skull. I was unable to think clearly and had difficulty focusing on anything for more than a short time. I was off work for a full year; even then, I struggled to get back in the swing of things. But with physical therapy, sheer determination and by the grace of God, I recovered fully.

I suffered my third brain hemorrhage on September 11, 2002. I was dizzy. I was weak. My vision was blurry and my hearing was impaired. I was unable to walk, drive, or work. Three and one-half months later, I returned to work; just ten months later I was back to normal.

People often walk up to me and say, "I can't believe you've had a brain hemorrhage and brain surgery. You look terrific!"

There were twenty-four things wrong with me after my hemorrhage on Christmas Day 2005, many of them quite serious. After nine months, I have recovered from all but two of these problems (see below).

Neurological Damage Christmas Day 2005	Status August 9, 2006
Double vision in left eye	Recovered
Blurred vision in left eye	Much improved
Unable to close left eye	Recovered (This one took a full nine months)
Droopy left eye	Recovered with eye surgery
Difficulty chewing food	Recovered
Difficulty swallowing food	Recovered
Loss of taste	Recovered
Physical weakness	Recovered
Lack of stamina	Recovered
Balance & equilibrium problems—unable to stand or walk without falling	Recovered
Difficulty with bowels	Recovered
Difficulty urinating	Recovered
Difficulty speaking	Recovered
Involuntary muscle twitching	Recovered
Severe headaches	Recovered

Sensitivity to light	Recovered
Sensitivity to noise	Recovered
Spacey feeling—like I wasn't all here	Recovered
Acute vertigo	Recovered
Deaf in left ear	Recovered with hearing aid
Droopy face	Recovered
Bloodshot & irritated left eye	Recovered
Blurry vision in left eye	Recovered
Unable to smile	Not recovered

And I am still working on that not being able to smile thing.

The point is, my nerve damage was only temporary. You might say, "But it took a year for you to recover. That's a long time." And you would be right. But I did recover, and a year is, after all, only temporary—a brief moment in time.

I learned this after my first brain surgery. I was having a difficult time recovering and was worried that I may never recover; I also worried that I wouldn't be able to work and support my family. I went to see my pastor. I was whining about why this had happened to me. I was fretting about whether I would ever get better. I asked him for guidance. The conversation went something like this:

Father Bob: How old are you?

Les: Forty-three.

Father Bob: How has your life been up to this point?

Les: Very good.

Father Bob: You have had forty-three years of good living, and now you're having a few months of hard times?

Les: Yes.

Father Bob: This too shall pass.

Good point. First, it put the few months of suffering into perspective by realizing that it was just a small portion of an otherwise good life. Second, I realized that the suffering (whatever it was) would pass. I began to realize that it was only temporary.

I worked hard, and I was determined. I kept my faith strong and prayed a lot. As a result, my neurological damage has always been temporary. And, it's the dinosaur principle—in a few million years or so, no one will care.

One of the keys to my recoveries was believing and knowing that my physical paralysis, weakness, lack of sight, lack of hearing, constant headaches, and everything else was only temporary, then working hard to make sure that was the case. Sometimes temporary lasted a year or more, but it was always temporary.

THE GOOD, THE BAD & THE UGLY

"You cannot go around and keep score. If you keep score on the good things and the bad things, you'll find out that you're a very miserable person. God gave man the ability to forget, which is one of the greatest attributes you have. Because if you remember everything that's happened to you, you generally remember that which is the most unfortunate."

Hubert H. Humphrey
U.S. politician (1911–1978)

The title of this chapter is the good, the bad and the ugly. You've already gotten the message, I hope, that I believe strongly in focusing on the good stuff. Most of this book has been about the remarkable recoveries I've made from very bad illnesses.

I've talked about going from being a bed-ridden, neurologically damaged human being to becoming a fully functional person again. I've talked about celebrating the small and large steps along the way.

You've also heard me tell you that it is better to talk and think about those things that are still good and the things that are getting better—start with the fact that you are still alive—than to dwell on what is bad. And as your recovery progresses, you will have more good things to talk about than bad things.

So you already know how important I believe it is for someone who is sick to stay positive—to concentrate on the good and not dwell on the bad.

But being sick is not all positive. Suffering is suffering, and bad and ugly things go along with it. So enough about being positive. Let's talk about some of the bad and the ugly times of my illnesses.

The Ugly: My First Brain Hemorrhage

This occurred in 1990 while my family and I were living in England. I was in the third month of a rigid diet and exercise program when I decided to play one-on-three basketball with my sons. I was the one, they were the three. I was forty-one years old. They were teenagers.

If this sounds like a bad idea, it was. Looking back, I now realize that my body was physically weakened from eating fewer than 1000 calories per day for weeks. Hunger had literally kept me awake at night, and I was tired from lack of sleep. So in my weakened and tired condition, I challenged three boys, less than half my age, to a strenuous basketball game.

Immediately after the game I began to feel dizzy and light-headed—I attributed it to my crash diet. I had been starving myself for weeks, so it was bound to make me a bit wobbly. Right?

I went to bed that evening still not feeling well. I awoke

in the middle of the night with the worst nausea and headache I had ever imagined possible.

My bed became my domain. I was physically unable to move. I laid there for days in pain and agony. I thought I had over-dieted and as soon as I got my strength back, I'd be fine. Macho me!

When I didn't get better, I saw a myriad of doctors in the socialized medical system, none of whom properly diagnosed my condition. By the grace of God, I recovered on my own. The outcome was great, but the getting there was ugly.

The Bad: My Fourth Brain Hemorrhage

My fourth hemorrhage occurred on Christmas Day, 2005. Now that's a Christmas I won't soon forget. My three sons and my daughter-in-law had all flown from Ohio to Texas to celebrate Christmas with my wife, Sharon, and me. I awoke Christmas morning with severe neurological damage to the left side of my face. I spent Christmas Day 2005 in the emergency room and the Intensive Care Unit of the hospital.

I was diagnosed with a bleed in the pons area of the brainstem. More than six weeks lapsed between my hemorrhage and surgery.

During these six weeks, I felt as though I was on an emotional roller coaster ride. I was gradually climbing the highest hill, holding my breath and closing my eyes while I was waiting for *risky* brain surgery on the downhill slope. If I could just get to the top of the highest hill, the trip down would be really, really fast and it would all be over. But I couldn't get to the top of the hill. The roller coaster was going slower and slower as it made its climb. I wanted desperately for surgery to be over and done with.

I knew that there would be other, less steep hills to negotiate before the ride was over, and that there would be sharp turns and other scary things to contend with—but I just wanted to get the surgery over and done.

I became very anxious. I was losing one to two pounds a day—every day—just worrying. All in all, I lost twenty-five pounds in three and one-half weeks. I wasn't sleeping due to worry. I was getting neurologically worse, not better. I couldn't leave my home. I couldn't watch television or read a book all because of nerve damage. I was going stir crazy. I became an emotional wreck. My doctor prescribed anti-anxiety medication to calm me down and it worked—sometimes.

I was frightened about surgery. After all, everyone kept telling me how risky it was. Yet, at the same time, I wanted the surgery to be over. As the weeks went by and nothing happened, I decided that one way not to be frightened about surgery was *not* to have surgery. It was my choice, wasn't it? If I decided not to have surgery, there would be nothing to be afraid of. That was it. I would decline the option for surgery. The source of my fear would be eliminated. Problem solved!

Boy, was this stinkin' thinkin'! Fortunately, my family, friends, and doctor convinced me that declining surgery was not a good option.

I realized that this was not my decision—I needed to consider the concerns of my wife, my children, and my many friends. These important people didn't want to see my neurological condition continue to worsen over the years due to lack of surgery. These important people wanted me to get better—not worse. The funny thing was that once I took them into account and once surgery was finally scheduled, I became much calmer and at peace with what was happening.

Note: It turns out that the reason my surgery was delayed was to give my brain time to stop bleeding and for the swelling to go down. This would make the operation less risky. I just wish someone had told me that.

The Ugly: The Infamous Four-hour Dental Exam

It was a little less than two months after my last surgery when my wife and I decided to get our teeth cleaned and checked. I walked into the dentist's office intending to have a dental exam, and I walked out with an exam, x-rays, cleaning, and three crowns. I spent a little more than four hours in the dentist's chair that day. Afterward, I was exhausted, and my head was pounding with pain.

I started with the cleaning and exam. Then the dental assistant decided to do x-rays. No big deal. When she came to me with the results of my x-rays, she informed me that I would need three crowns. "Now, these don't all have to be done today, but if you are agreeable, we *can* do them all today and save you the trouble of having to come back." Somehow this sounded so appealing. In a weakened, obviously brain damaged moment, I agreed. Not smart! It took me weeks to fully recover from the infamous four-hour dental exam.

As I write this chapter, I realize it has been seven and a half months since I had surgery. I have improved greatly since the infamous four-hour dental exam. I checked my calendar, and guess what? I have another dentist appointment tomorrow. I will *not* be getting three crowns tomorrow. I will not be getting even one crown tomorrow. You know, getting a cleaning, exam, x-rays, and three crowns in one trip to the dentist just doesn't sound like a smart thing to do—even for someone who is perfectly healthy. What was I thinking?

The Bad: My First Brain Surgery

I was experiencing some tingling and numbness in my left arm and leg. It wasn't severe and really only surfaced after I exercised, worked in the yard, or done some other strenuous activity. I recognized that these were symptoms similar to those I had experienced eighteen months earlier, while living abroad. Only they were not nearly so severe. So I went to the doctor, and she ordered an MRI.

I was supposed to schedule an appointment with a neurologist two days later to get the results, but before I got around to it, I received a panic phone call from the doctor telling me I needed to come to the hospital immediately!

After reviewing the test results, she scheduled me for an appointment with a neurosurgeon the very next day. I remember thinking, *A neurosurgeon does surgery, right? Am I going to have brain surgery? This can't be happening.*

I told my boss. He told me that I shouldn't worry about my job—they would hold the fort down while I recovered. Great!

I remember driving several months after surgery—which in retrospect I shouldn't have been doing. I got to the middle of what should have been a familiar intersection near my home—I was confused I didn't know where I was. I couldn't remember whether to turn left, right, or go straight ahead. I had successfully negotiated this intersection many times before, but on that day, at that moment, I just didn't know what to do. My brain was foggy.

Then, just I was wondering how in the world I could return to work with this foggy brain of mine—which for all I knew was a permanent condition—the phone rang. It was my boss. He was sorry to tell me that my job had been eliminated. He explained that not only had my job been eliminated, but that the 2,900 jobs at our company headquarters had been cut in a massive downsizing. This was a lot to digest.

- I had been diagnosed with a severe hemorrhage.
- It had happened eighteen months prior.
- I was told I was lucky to be alive.
- I had had brain surgery.
- I was struggling to recover after being overmedicated.
- I lost my job.

And, all of this had happened in a period of just three or four months.

I went on to recover on a good disability package. I got a big severance check and found a new and better job. Do you see a pattern here? A good outcome but a bad experience, once again.

So the message is that not every moment during a serious illness is good. In fact many bad and ugly times happen during serious illnesses. I've certainly had my share.

BE AN INSPIRATION TO OTHERS

"If you are ever going to see a rainbow, you have got to stand a little rain."

Unknown

I recently had lunch with an old friend. It had been more than seven months since I underwent surgery, and although my friend was aware of what I had gone through, we had not seen each other for more than a year. Although I had improved a lot, I still looked a little funny.

We spoke briefly about my illness and the possibility that I could have additional episodes in the future. The next day, I received the following email from him:

Les,

I was visiting with my six-year-old son last night about my day. I talked about meeting you and I shared a bit of your story. He paused for a moment and said, "Dad, can I pray for Mr. Duncan?" Of course, I said yes—so know you're being lifted up around our household.

My son's name is Clayton, he prayed out loud with me

last night as he was going to sleep and he prayed, "That Mr. Duncan would be all better." He goes to a private Christian school and they do popcorn prayer and he told me he would pray for you in his class too. (He's in a private school and they pray daily out loud in class).

Have a great day!

Scott

Well, knowing that Clayton is praying for me, how can I *not* have a great day? This bit of news really lifted me up. It is the latest in a long list of inspirations that I've been to others and others have been to me.

Similarly, my wife's brother has six children. One of the first get-well cards I received after my last surgery was from these four nieces and two nephews. They all wrote a note saying they were praying for me. My five-year-old nephew told me, "I'm praying for you, Uncle Les." My eight-year-old niece said, "My entire second grade class prays for you everyday." Fortunately for me, God listens to children.

I am still amazed at the number of people who come up to me and say, "You have been a real inspiration to me and my family." It seems to me that nearly everyone is either really sick or knows someone who is really sick, and these folks tell me that they have used me as an example of someone who has successfully survived not one but several serious illnesses.

They talk about my courage. My optimism. My determination. They talk about my positive attitude. But, most of all, they talk about me being a living example of someone who was in pretty bad shape, but refused to allow that to be the end state.

I don't know how many people have come up to me and

said, "My brother [cousin, friend, etc.] has been diagnosed with a brain problem, and they are scared and confused. I've told them your story of survival, and it really helped." Some have even asked me to visit their friends and relatives so they can see a walking, living example of someone who has survived a similar illness and is doing just fine. I relish these opportunities.

These days, I bring a photo of myself when I was at my worst. I look so much better now, and the comparison of the before photo is startling.

I volunteer by visiting the sick in the hospital. I talk, listen, and pray with patients who are sick. I give them Holy Communion. But most of all, I let them see a person who has been very sick—several times in my life—and has recovered. They tell me I give them hope, and that I provide them with inspiration.

In my case, I had a chance to be an inspiration to my youngest son, Mike, who also suffers from the same vascular malformation condition that I do. I passed along the bad genes.

He had his first hemorrhage when he was only twenty-two years old; his second hemorrhage and brain surgery occurred when he was twenty-three. He found inspiration in the fact that I had previously recovered fully from two hemorrhages and a surgery.

There were remarkable similarities between his first episodes and my last episodes. So when I suffered my last hemorrhage and underwent my last surgery, he provided inspiration for me.

His first hemorrhage was in his brain stem, and he suffered (temporary) severe damage to both eyes. My last hemorrhage was in the brainstem and also affected my vision.

His first surgery was to remove the malformed veins that caused his brainstem to bleed, as was my last surgery. His first episodes were much more critical than my first episodes. For me to see how this brave young man dealt with his catastrophic illnesses was a huge inspiration for me to get through mine.

I remember when he was lying in the hospital bed awaiting surgery. His eyes were bugged out of his head due to fluid and swelling in the brain. They had drilled a hole in his skull bone and inserted a drain to get rid of as much fluid as possible. He was confined to bed. He felt terrible.

He said many things to my wife and I. For instance, he told us he was confident he would be all right. He told us he knew his recovery would take time. But the thing he said that meant the most to me was, "Dad, you know this isn't your fault. Don't worry about the genes thing." I remember how sensitive and astute he was to take this burden from me. What an inspiration.

Many people prayed for me during my illnesses. Hundreds of people prayed for me, some of whom I didn't know personally. But many I did know. Some hadn't been to church in years. Others hadn't prayed for anything or anybody in a long time. My illness inspired them to realize that faith was important in their life.

Seeing and hearing about my near miraculous comebacks reinforced and rekindled their religious beliefs. They could see that their prayers had worked. My recovery inspired them to return to church and to return to prayer as a way of life.

So, be an inspiration to others. As Robert Louis Stevenson said, "Keep your fears to yourself, but share your inspiration with others."

DO I HAVE COOTIES?

"A man is known by the company he avoids."

Anonymous

Many friends, neighbors, and co-workers kept in close touch with me during my illnesses. I received a plethora of phone calls, cards, letters, flowers, plants, candy, and one person even sent me Grater's ice cream shipped all the way from Ohio. By the way, if you have never had Grater's ice cream, you don't know what you're missing.

I also received many visitors. Friends and relatives visited me in the Intensive Care Unit of the hospitals. Other friends and family visited me in my home immediately following surgery. One friend came the first evening I was home from the hospital.

But many others avoided me altogether. People that I had known for years and co-workers with whom I had been close stayed away from me like I had the plague. I didn't hear from them, and I didn't see them. I began to think that maybe I had cooties.

"Cooties" is a slang word used primarily by North

American children to refer to a fictitious contagious disease or condition. It usually presents along gender lines, as in Kevin K. Ford, "stay away from those girls or you might get cooties![5]

Originally, the term implied body lice, but over time this became generalized first to any sort of lice, including head lice, then later to purely imaginary stand-ins for just about anything that is considered repulsive.[6]

Well, whatever it is I was convinced I must have it. Why else would people be avoiding me? I realized folks were busy. I realized they couldn't put their lives on hold to give me a call or pay me a visit. But I was laid up for months. It just seemed to me that sometime during those months, they could have made some time for me. How selfish this must sound, but it was important to me to know that my closest friends and relatives were thinking about me and cared.

I've seen a number of these men and women now that I'm up and around; being the brazen, bold, no punches-barred kind of guy that I am, I've asked them directly, "Why didn't you come see me when I was sick?" It turns out there were a number of reasons.

The most frequent answer I got was, "I didn't know you were allowed to have visitors." Or, "I didn't know you wanted to have visitors." They went on to explain that they thought about me often and that I was in their daily prayers, but they just weren't sure how sick I really was. They didn't know whether the doctor would allow them to visit me and even if he was allowing visitors, they didn't know if I felt up to seeing them. After all, I *was* in pretty bad shape.

Another answer I got was, "I couldn't bear the thought of seeing you when you were in such bad shape." They went on to say that they had heard from others that I was weak, fragile, and disabled. The Les Duncan they knew was strong, vibrant, and active. They didn't know if I would ever be the same, and they simply didn't want to remember me as anything less than the Les Duncan they had come to know and love.

A third answer I got was, "I just don't deal well with sick people. Seeing someone who is really sick just drags me down, emotionally." I certainly understand this. When I was younger, I was lucky enough to know all of my grandparents and to have them with me for a good part of my life. My maternal grandfather died when I was thirty-two years old. I watched as all my grandparents got very sick, and I remember how difficult it was for me to visit them in the hospital when they were dying. Emotionally, it was very hard for me to see them in such a weakened condition.

A fourth answer I got was, "I simply didn't think you were that sick." They knew I was positive and that I was determined to recover fully, and they didn't want to treat me as though I was in some kind of catastrophic situation by suddenly showing up at my doorstep. "If I had known how bad you were, I would have been there at your side," they said.

Finally, when I asked someone why they hadn't been in touch, the answer I got was, "I didn't want to bother you." They explained that my weekly email updates talked about frequent naps, therapist appointments, doctors' visits, exercises, and other things that appeared to be taking up all my time. They just didn't want to interfere with my routine.

So there may be a few people who avoid you when you

are sick for a variety of reasons. Here is how I recommend you approach this issue:

1. Let others know when your doctor has cleared you for visitors. Doctors are protective of their patients, and rightfully so, sometimes keeping them away from the general masses to avoid unneeded excitement and the potential exposure to germs for some time period after major surgery. You or someone close to you has to give the "green light" for visitors. Once this is done, you won't be able to keep them away.

2. Let others know when *you* are ready for visitors. I, for one, just wasn't physically or emotionally able to accept visitors for a few weeks following a major episode. Use your email communication chain to let everyone know when you are ready for folks to come see you.

3. Make the first move. If there is someone you really want to see or talk to, don't sit around waiting for the phone or doorbell to ring—call him or her. Have a long chat. Invite them over.

4. Set up visiting hours for your home. It's true that I was pretty busy resting, exercising, and going to doctor appointments after my illnesses. But I tried to leave one weekday open for myself. In retrospect, I should have let people know that I was home all day on Fridays, and that day would be a good time to visit.

5. Let them know what to expect. The final piece of advice I would give is to let everyone know what

to expect. I was seeing folks that had not seen me since I suffered nerve damage. I didn't look physically well, and I didn't get around very well. While in the hospital, I was connected to many hoses and wires and to machines that constantly beeped and flashed signals. It was important to "warn" these people, in advance, that I was not my old self yet. No surprises.

I will conclude this chapter by talking about a related issue—embarrassment. After my first brain surgery, I was embarrassed that I had gotten so sick. I wasn't the father and husband that I had once been. I couldn't work. I couldn't drive. I figured most people probably pitied me.

I had also squarely played the blame game and concluded that everything was my fault. Had I only taken better care of myself....Had I not played basketball with my three teenage sons....I was ashamed that my physical condition had deteriorated and that I wasn't the man I used to be. I hadn't yet learned to be confident and positive about my recovery.

As a result, I didn't want any visitors. I shut myself out from the rest of the world, and I only allowed a few close friends and family to make contact. *What people must think of me now?* I thought.

Then I talked to a friend and told him how I felt. He pointed out that I was recovering nicely. "Yes, thank you very much," I said. Then he asked me the following question, "If I had gone through what you've been through, and were recovering as well as you are, what would you think about me?" Without thinking, I said, "I'd be really proud of you and happy for you." "So what makes you think we're not all really proud of you and happy for you then?" Enough said.

BAD THINGS
DO HAPPEN TO
GOOD PEOPLE

"If you can imagine it, you can achieve it. If
you can dream it, you can become it."

William Arthur Ward

The fact is—stuff happens. Bad stuff happens. And yes, bad
stuff happens to good people. I am living proof of that.

I am a good person. I am a good husband, a good father,
a good son, a good friend, and a good employee. I believe in
God and cherish my faith. I visit the sick. I give generously
to my church and other charities. I am kind to others. I am
a big tipper. When I meet someone—even a stranger—I
strive to make his or her day better, no matter how brief the
encounter. Could I be a better person? Of course I could.
We can all be better. But, all in all, I think I'm a pretty good
person.

Yet I have had four brain hemorrhages and two brain
surgeries. There is no doubt that these were bad things. So I
am proof that bad things happen to good people.

And why does it seem that when it rains it pours? Following my first brain surgery, I lost my job. This devastated me. Following my last brain surgery, it seemed as though my whole house began to fall apart. Windows needed to be replaced, electrical lights and fans needed repair, and the plumbing broke.

It is natural to ask why? Why do bad things happen to good people? As I said in an earlier chapter, it is counterproductive to play the blame game. After deep reflection I have concluded that stuff just happens.

A catastrophic illness is a life-changing experience. So just think about what changes six catastrophic illnesses have made in my life.

I definitely changed for the better after my first brain hemorrhage. I changed even more after my first brain surgery. I kept changing up through my last hemorrhage and brain surgery. Today, I am a much better person than I was in 1998 when I first became sick. Again, I would like to think I was always a good person, but I have become an even better person as a result of my suffering.

For instance, Ken, one of my employees, suffered a brain aneurysm just a few months after he started working for me. His nerve damage was significant, and he was worried about his job and the potential lack of income. I talked with him and his wife and conveyed the following messages. 1) Don't worry about your job just focus on getting better. 2) When you do get better, your job will be waiting for you, no matter how long it takes.

A few months later, I was attending a company function and the wife of one of my managers came up to me and said, "I think it is wonderful what you are doing for Ken. He is so much more at ease knowing that he doesn't have to worry about his job. What a blessing it is that you have gone through similar experiences and are so understanding."

Well, I think I would have taken the same approach regardless of my personal situation. But would I?

So why *do* bad things happen to good people? Perhaps it is because suffering makes us better human beings. In my case, I began to value things that I had previously taken for granted—such as the ability to walk and see. I started doing things I had previously postponed—like writing books and going on vacations. I began to care more about others and less about myself. My illnesses have inspired me to visit the sick in the hospital. I began to live life as if there was no tomorrow. And I have grown closer to God.

During my recoveries, I've tried hard not to feel sorry for myself. Rather I've focused on all the positives in my life. Yes, I have suffered some nerve damage. Yes, my illnesses have placed my life on hold for months at a time. But I have a fabulous wife who loves me very much. I have three wonderful sons and a great daughter-in-law. I have enough money to live comfortably. I still have my ability to walk, talk, and care for myself. And, I am still alive.

Life has dealt me a basket of lemons, but I have done my best to make them into lemonade. I have done my best not to let these bad things leave a sour taste in my mouth. I have worked hard to allow them to make me a better person.

In my younger days, I was often described as brash. Today, I am described as a nice guy or a good man. When my oldest son was interviewed for his job, he was asked what person he most admired in this world. His answer was his father—me. I take this all as proof that the bad things that have happened in my life have indeed made me a better person.

THERE IS NO PLACE LIKE HOME

"Mid pleasures and palaces though we may roam, be it ever so humble, there's no place like home."

John Howard Payne

Dorothy (Judy Garland) told us how important going home was in the classic movie *The Wizard of Oz*. She stood in the presence of the Mighty Wizard, clicked the heels of her ruby red slippers as she repeated the mantra, "There's no place like home. There's no place like home. There's no place like home."

Recall that Dorothy had been swept up in a Kansas tornado and ended up in the bizarre Land of Oz. When I return to Kansas (my original home) for a visit, I see all sorts of Wizard of Oz souvenirs. There are dolls—Dorothy, the scarecrow, the lion, the tin man, and even Toto the dog. There are calendars, notepads, collages, and other Oz memorabilia. But my favorite item is a coffee mug with the following saying:

Dear Dorothy,
Hate Oz,
Took the shoes, Find your own way home!
Toto

When I visit the sick in hospital, no matter what the ailment, no matter how serious their illness, they all share the same desire—to go home.

When I visit with these folks, I always try to get them to smile or laugh. All I have to do is ask them, "When are you going home?" Their faces light up and they begin to smile as they respond, "tomorrow" or "next week." The closer it is to their return to home date, the bigger they smile. There's no place like home!

I have a great deal of respect for those who work in the healthcare industry. They are good people who provide a priceless service. And they really *try* to make a hospital stay pleasant.

In recent years hospitals have come to realize that they face competition from other hospitals. They have come to realize that we—the patients—are their customers, and that they need to provide good customer service to their patients/customers. Most hospitals are now very service oriented and the staff will do whatever they can to make their patients/customers happy. So the hospitalization experience is so much better today than it was a decade ago.

But hospitals are still not fun, and they are still not home. This is not a criticism, it is a fact. I, like the majority of patients, found hospital food marginal. The hospital—not me—was in control of my life and my schedule. It seemed that someone was always in my room to take my vital signs, give me medications, check my blood sugar, check my neurological functions, and who knows what else. They even did these things in the middle of the night. Not once, but twice in the middle of the night. Then the resident—who I am convinced must have lived and slept in the hospital—stopped by around at 5:30 a.m. to check in on me. So basically I got no sleep. It's no wonder I looked forward to getting out of there and back home.

And, you don't have to be hospitalized to miss home sweet home. Virtually anytime I am away from home I'm anxious to get back. I traveled a lot on business before I retired. Business travel can be fun and exciting, but after a couple of days, I always found myself longing to see my wife and to sleep in my own bed in my own home. Vacations are also good. No matter how much fun I have on a vacation, I'm happy to return home. There is just nothing akin to sleeping on my own pillow and in my own Select Comfort Sleep Number Bed (my sleep number is 45).

Home is a safe place—a safe haven where I feel secure. Somewhere where I feel sheltered from the outside world. Home is a place where I can seek refuge from my problems. Going home brought with it a sense of normalcy that I longed for.

But then there's the other side of the coin. When I was sick, the hospital was also a safe place. In spite of the many things that made the hospital an unpleasant place to be, the hospital was a place where I was surrounded by doctors, nurses, and other health professionals who were trained to keep me well. If something *should* happen, what better place to be than in the hospital?

Following my first brain surgery, I was recovering slower than I expected. I had difficulty thinking, and I seemed to be getting worse, not better. I became anxious, and I longed to be readmitted to the hospital until someone could figure out what was wrong with me. The hospital, I kept telling myself, was where I wanted to be.

Yet there is simply no place like home. It is safe. It is secure. It is familiar. And you, the patient, are in control of your life. You—not the hospital—decide when and what to eat. You decide when to sleep or nap. You sleep in your own bed and watch your favorite television programs or videos. Hospitals are for sick people—going home from them gives you the sense of being on the road to recovery. There is no place like home!

THE POWER
OF PRAYER

"Pray any way you like, so long as you do pray. You can pray the way your mother taught you; you can use a prayer book. Sometimes it takes courage to pray; but it is possible to pray, and necessary to pray. Whether from memory or a book or just in thought, it is all the same."

Pope John Paul II

There is nothing like a good trauma to get you close to God. There is nothing like a near death experience to get you praying. Even those who don't actively practice their faith will turn to prayer during a critical illness. And yes, even those who don't believe in God will start praying when faced with a catastrophe.

Prayer is one of the best free gifts we receive. There is no cost, but a lot of reward. Make sure you pray believing that God will answer. Especially when you are sick.

I prayed a lot when I was sick. Some days the only thing I *could* do was lay in bed and pray—I just wasn't physically able to do anything else. I still pray a lot. I pray the rosary every day, plus I say morning prayers, mealtime prayers, and bedtime prayers. I pray aloud, and I pray in silence. God hears me either way.

Plus, I was very lucky. Many people prayed for me when I was sick, and most are still praying for me today. Friends, co-workers, family, and even people I didn't know all prayed for me. I am amazed that, to this day, I will meet someone I haven't seen for years, and who was not on my communication list, and they will say to me, "I heard about your illness, and I have been praying for you."

I love to visit the sick in the hospital. I talk with them about their illnesses. I always pray that my mere presence provides them hope and inspiration. I also pray for them and encourage them to pray with me. Often, they ask me to come back and pray some more with them on another day. That's really cool!

One of the most frequent requests I get is, "Will you teach me how to pray?" The best I can do is to teach them how *I* pray, and hope that is good enough.

The first thing I suggest is that they talk to God like they would a friend. Don't worry about being formal, just start by saying "Hello, God." I try to make my prayers a conversation with God. Not a one-side conversation, but a two-way communication. It is remarkable what God will tell you if you just pause to listen.

I follow a basic outline:

1. *I ask for forgiveness.* Oftentimes, I do, say, or think something that is offensive to God. I try not to, but I do. It is important to me to reconcile myself with God before I move on to other issues. Then I pause to see what God has to say to me.

2. *I thank God for all His blessings.* When I was sick, sometimes things seemed pretty grim. But there was always a lot to be thankful for. When I pray, I thank God for His many blessings, and I do it with *sincere gratitude.*

    a. The gift of life. Life is precious, and we must never take it for granted.

    b. My good health. I thank him for my good spiritual health and the strong faith I have that he has and will continue to help me. I thank him for my good emotional health and my positive attitude about myself. And I thank him for my good physical health. I tell him how grateful I am that the neurological damage I've suffered has not been severe and has been mostly temporary.

    c. For keeping us all safe from radical terrorists— the people in this world who hate us because we are Americans and who want to kill us. I thank God for protecting us from these evil people.

    d. For my family and marriage. I thank God for my wife, my sons, my daughter-in-law, and my daughter-in-law to be.

    e. For the power of prayer and the many people who pray for me. For the privilege to pray for others in need.

    f. For my retirement.

    g. For my many friends and family who provide me with love and support.

3. *I ask God's blessing for others.* I pray for my wife and

sons, my parents and siblings, my wife's family. I pray for all those who are sick, especially those who are suffering with a catastrophic illness, and those who are homebound, hospital bound, wheelchair bound, or bed bound. And for those who are unable to care for themselves without assistance. I pray for our priests and religious leaders, for our President and the leaders of other nations around the world— that the Holy Spirit may guide them in their actions and deeds. I pray for our servicemen and service-women serving our country. I pray for those in special need—those who are hungry and homeless, for example. And I always have a list of a dozen or so people who I know personally that have special needs, who have asked me to pray for them.

4. *I pray for myself.* It never occurred to me to pray for myself until I was in the hospital one time awaiting surgery and a Presbyterian minister came to visit me. She prayed with me for a while—a very powerful prayer. Then she said, "Are you praying for your-self everyday?" I told her I wasn't. And she snapped back, "Well, you should be. God wants to hear from you what you need from him." Great. So I pray for myself, but I always do it last.

I pray that I will be a good witness for God, and that others will experience His love in what I do and say. I ask that others may find inspiration in the fact that I have battled serious illness and won. I pray that God will continue to bless me with a full recovery. I pray that my wife and I will continue to love each other and that our family will remain close. I pray for a long, active, enjoyable retirement. And I pray that I will never have to live through another brain or spine hemorrhage or surgery again.

5. *I listen.* I begin by repeating one of my favorite phrases; "Speak now for your servant is listening." Then I clear my mind and listen to what God has to say. Prayer is very often much more a question of listening than speaking. Yes, we have something to say to God, but more importantly he has something to say to us.

One of my favorite Bible stories is from the Old Testament and is about Elijah listening to God. Allow me to paraphrase it as follows:

> Elijah, like most profits, was a hermit. He lived in the desert and in the mountains. The Bible tells us that Jezebel was hunting Elijah down, and she wanted to kill him. Elijah fled to the mountains.
>
> God told Elijah that He (God) would be passing by, so Elijah should prepare himself. So Elijah went into a cave, and the Bible tells us that a mighty storm came with thunder and lightning, and then a powerful earthquake followed.
>
> But God wasn't in the storm, and God wasn't in the earthquake. Then eventually a still, tiny voice was heard, and Elijah hid his face in his cloak because he knew that God was passing by.

The lesson here is that very often God doesn't come with a

great clap of thunder or a flash of lightning. Very often he comes in quiet, tiny moments. The voice of God is often soft and gentle like a light breeze.

Does God always listen to our prayers? Yes. Does he always answer our prayers? Yes. Sometimes we may not like the answer, but he does answer. We all have to remember that God sees the bigger picture. He knows better than we do what is best for us.

I believe that the best way to pray to God is by having a conversation with Him. Speaking to Him as a friend. And taking time to listen to what He has to say.

I also like to use a prayer book. The way I figure it, someone who is probably smarter and more dedicated than I am has taken the time to write some beautiful prayers, and I am certainly willing to take advantage of that.

A friend of mine sent me the following prayers during her daughter's recent illness. They are all from prayer books written by someone else, and they are all prayers for the sick. I use these often when I visit the sick in the hospital.

Prayer Before Surgery

Loving Father, I entrust (name) to Your care this day; guide with wisdom and skill the minds and hands of the medical people who minister in Your Name, and grant that every cause of illness be removed, that he/she be restored to soundness of health and learn to live in more perfect harmony with you and with those around him/her. We ask this through Jesus Christ. Amen.[7]

Prayer after a surgery

Blessed Savior, I thank you that this operation is safely past, and now I rest in Your abiding presence, relaxing every tension, releasing every care and anxiety, receiving more and more of Your healing life into every part of my being. In moments of pain I turn to you for strength, in times of loneliness I feel Your loving nearness. Grant that Your life and love and joy may flow through me for the healing of others in Your name. Amen.[8]

Prayer for healing

Lord, You invite all who are burdened to come to You. Allow Your healing hand to heal (name). Touch her/his soul with Your compassion for others. Touch her/his heart with Your courage and infinite love for all. Touch her/his mind with Your wisdom, that her/his mouth may always proclaim Your praise. Teach her/him to reach out to You in her/him need, and help her/him to lead others to You by her/his example. Most loving Heart of Jesus, bring (name) health in body and spirit that she may serve You with all her/his strength. Touch gently this life that You have created, now and forever. Amen.[9]

Another prayer for healing

O God who are the only source of health and healing, the spirit of calm and the central peace of this universe, grant to (name) such a consciousness of Your indwelling and surrounding presence that she/he may permit you to give her/him health and strength and peace, through Jesus Christ our Lord. Amen.[10]

Prayer for healing

Lord, look upon (name) with eyes of mercy, may Your healing hand rest upon her/him, may Your life-giving powers flow into every cell of her/his body and into the depths of her/his soul, cleansing, purifying, restoring her/him to wholeness and strength for service in Your Kingdom. Amen.[11]

Prayer of the sick

Dear Jesus, Healer of the Sick, I turn to You in this time of illness. Alleviate my worry and sorrow with Your gentle love and grant me the grace the strength to accept this burden. I place my worries in Your hands. I place myself in Your care and humbly ask that You restore me to health again. Above all, grant me the grace to acknowledge Your holy will and know that You love me and are with me in this my most difficult time. Amen.[12]

Prayer during sickness

May I have peace within today.
May I trust God that I am exactly where I am meant to be.
May I not forget the infinite possibilities that are born of faith.
May I use those gifts that I have received, and pass on the love that I have been given.
May I be content knowing that I am a child of God.
May I let His presence settle into my bones, and allow my soul the freedom to sing, dance, praise and love.[13]

Unfailing prayer to St. Anthony

O Holy St. Anthony, gentlest of Saints, your love for God and Charity for His creatures, made you worthy, when on earth, to possess miraculous powers. Encouraged by this thought, I implore you to obtain for me (request). O gentle and loving St. Anthony, whose heart was ever full of human sympathy, whisper my petition into the ears of the sweet Infant Jesus, who loved to be folded in your arms; and the gratitude of my heart will ever be yours. Amen.[14]

And here is a simple prayer I made up during my recovery:

Prayer during recovery

Dear God, Dear Jesus, Dear Holy Spirit;
Thank you for the recovery that I have made so far and
Please continue to bless me with Your divine healing power

I believe strongly in the power of prayer—and not just in times of illness. Let me conclude by telling you a brief story about something that happened to me during my last illness.

It was February 9, 2006—the date of my last brain surgery. A small army was praying for me. Knowing that made me feel so secure and so peaceful as I prepared for the event.

My wife received a phone call the day before from Jerry, one of my co-workers, who explained that the great people I worked with would be holding a prayer luncheon during the same time I was having surgery. He asked Sharon to call him as soon as she knew something so he could pass the news along to those who were attending—some 150 people. As they rolled me into surgery, I said to my wife, "Don't forget to call Jerry." She assured me that he would be her first call.

I was undergoing surgery while my wife sat, awaiting

word, in the surgical waiting area. Hours later, the doctor emerged to tell her that everything had gone well and that I was going to be fine. As promised she immediately called Jerry with the good news. Jerry said, "Thank God. You know, you called just as we concluded our prayer and said Amen." Right on queue. Everyone cheered loudly. That was really cool! I still get chills up and down my spine just thinking of this!

So whether you are sick or not, take time to pray every day. If you aren't sick, thank God for your good health. Don't take it for granted. If you are sick, pray for your recovery. Amen.

LOOK FOR THE GREATER GOOD

"A wise man should consider that health is the greatest of human blessings, and learn how by his own thought to derive benefit from his illnesses."

Hippocrates
Greek physician (460BC–377 BC)

There is only one reason why our loving God would permit evil, pain, and suffering—for a greater good. Notice I said permit—not cause. Most Christians believe that the greatest evil ever committed was the crucifixion and death of Jesus Christ. Yet from this greatest evil also came the greatest good—the forgiveness of the sins of all mankind and the promise of everlasting life.

I know a woman who suffered a severe neurological disease that temporarily caused her to be paralyzed. After six months, she was still a bit frail and in a wheelchair, but she had regained most of her muscular function. She told me she had taken her first few steps on her own just days earlier. She also said, "Les, there is a reason why God allows us to suffer. It's so we can go on to tell others about it and to show them our miraculous recoveries." Amen to that!

Take 9/11/2001. The day when radical Muslims flew jumbo jets into the World Trade Center, the Pentagon, and a field in Pennsylvania—the most tragic attack on American soil ever! More innocent people died in these attacks than at Pearl Harbor. More than 3,000 innocent people were slaughtered.

I, like many Americans, first learned that something was wrong early that morning. The rumor was that one of the World Trade Center towers in New York was on fire. I gathered with co-workers around a television set, and we watched while a jumbo jet plowed into the second tower. Unbelievably on live TV! We subsequently watched as both towers came down—first one and then the other.

Why was God allowing this to happen? Such pain. Such suffering. Such evil. All of which was being inflicted, ironically, in the name of Ala—God himself. Father John Corapi points out that this tragedy brought about a greater good. In the words of this wise man, Father John:

On Monday our country was deeply divided. We had just experienced one of the closest presidential races in our country's history, and we were arguing and fighting about inane and inconsequential things. On Tuesday, all of this took a back seat to the events of 9/11 and we were all lined up giving blood.

On Monday children couldn't pray in schools. On Tuesday you couldn't find a school where they weren't praying.

On Monday and before, there were dozens of abortions performed every day in New York City. On Tuesday there weren't any–for a while. Planned parenthood had to give abortions away to drum up business.

The pornography guys almost went out of business.

Priests from all over the country reported that lines for confession were longer than ever.

Churches were packed from that weekend on.

Young people who had been satisfied to live together and postpone marriage to a more convenient time became engaged and scheduled wedding dates.[15]

I'm not suggesting that a serious illness compares with the events of 9/11 or the crucifixion of Jesus Christ, but the principle is the same. A greater good can come from all suffering, pain, and illness. Just look for it.

In my case, my last illness forced me to retire early from a very successful business career. But on the flip side, I am retired. My wife and I are traveling—something we love to do together. And I now have the time and talent to serve others. I do some teaching because I love helping children. I have written this book—a book that will hopefully inspire others who are experiencing serious illness. I do more volunteer work for my church and at the hospital.

My wife and I have been married for nearly forty years (she was a child bride). We have three wonderful, successful sons. We are each other's best friends. Our marriage has always been strong. However, our love for each other became even stronger as I went through my illnesses. I suffered. She took care of me. She literally placed her life on hold while she nursed me back to recovery—not once, but six times. She was my cheerleader on the many occasions when my spirits were down. She was the epitome of "in sickness and in health." All of this made me appreciate and love her even more. And seeing my suffering and my ultimate recovery made her appreciate and love me even more.

I continue to look for the greater good. I figure that God must have a special plan for me to have brought me through the pain and suffering of six serious illnesses.

For example, I know that many people prayed for me. Some of these returned to practicing their religion because of the miracle of prayer they saw in my recovery. Others told their sick friends about me and used me as an example of someone who had survived a serious illness, bringing hope and peace into the lives of their friends and relatives.

It took me a full year to recover from my first brain surgery. But, I recovered—almost fully. People who knew about my illness would walk up to me and say, "You look terrific!" One of my friends had a brother-in-law who was diagnosed with a brain tumor, and my friend used me as an example of someone who had survived a similar situation. She thanked me for the sake of her brother-in-law, who had hope because of my positive healing example.

Recently, I was on a vacation with my wife when another friend called me. Someone she knew had been diagnosed with brain cancer. She wanted to know what they should do. I forwarded them an early draft of this book and that helped. I also made recommendations on doctors, medical facilities, and treatment plans—based on my firsthand experiences. The doctors were very pessimistic about his recovery, so most of all I told them not to lose hope; if the doctor they were seeing couldn't help him, they should search for another one who could.

A member of my church had surgery to remove an aneurysm. She had strong faith, but she was also frightened. Again, I forwarded her an early manuscript of this book. Through the volunteer work I do at the hospital, I was able to visit her. I was a living, breathing example of someone who had survived and recovered from risky brain surgery. Her husband told me I inspired her.

When my son had his brain hemorrhages and his surgery, he had me as an example to look to. He knew that recovery was possible because he had witnessed mine firsthand. What a frightening experience it would have been for a twenty-three-year-old young man without this example. And, when I had my last surgery, he was with me to return the favor—providing hope and inspiration of his own.

So, it seems that I have become somewhat of an expert on brain problems, and that my remarkable recoveries have inspired others and provided much needed hope during difficult times. There is no greater good than to ease other people's suffering. There is no better purpose than to be a messenger of hope for those who are ailing.

STAY IN THE PRESENT MOMENT

"Learning to live in the present moment is part of the path of joy."

Sarah Ban Breathnach

What does it mean to "stay in the present moment"? Simply put, it means to focus on what is happening right here, right now, and *not* to dwell on what has already happened or worry about what may (or may not) happen in the future.

Sounds easy? Well, we all know from experience that it is not easy. In fact it can be very hard to stay in the present moment. The past and the future keep harassing us. The past with guilt—the future with worries.

Staying in the present moment was not easy for me even when I was not sick. I often found myself at home thinking of issues at work and, vice versa, thinking of home issues while at work. I still have difficulty focusing on what is happening at this moment in time. Occasionally I find my mind drifting to the past or looking anxiously to the future, and I have to deliberately bring my thinking back to the present.

When I was sick, my tendency to rehash the past inten-sified. I found myself going back, focusing on what I could have done to avoid a hemorrhage or a surgery. What if I hadn't played one-on-three basketball with my sons? What if I hadn't weakened my body from weeks on a starvation diet? What if I hadn't allowed my blood pressure to rise by worrying about my father? What if I hadn't attempted a whirlwind forty-eight-hour driving trip to Wichita, Kansas? What if I hadn't played golf, carrying my forty-five-pound bag on my back in ninety-eight-degree heat with 80% humidity? What if I had not let my job stress me out?

And, there was also the worrying about the future. What if I didn't get better? What if I couldn't drive or walk again? What if I couldn't work again? What if the surgeon's knife slipped?

It took me a while to learn that what had happened, had happened. What was done, was done. Nothing could be done to change the past. And what was yet to happen would also happen. Worrying about the past and the future was a waste of my time and energy.

In 1982 I left the Air Force and went to work for an oil and gas company in Cleveland, Ohio. I drove by myself from Wichita, Kansas, to Cleveland one Sunday. It was a long drive and I had my car radio tuned to a Christian broadcast (about all that was available). The preacher was talking about worrying. His point was that worrying does little good and can do a lot of harm.

He cited, as an example, the story of a man who was deeply in debt. The number of bills he had to pay over-whelmed this man. And he didn't have the money to pay them. Allow me to paraphrase his story.

So the man laid all his bills on the kitchen table and just sat there staring at them, worrying about it. He sat there for hours, thinking about what he had done to get himself in this predicament and worrying about what was going to happen to his life given his insurmountable debts. Guess what? Nothing changed.

After hours of second-guessing himself and fretting about the future, the bills still lay on the kitchen table unpaid. Worrying did him no good.

Perhaps he should have been out finding a second job? Perhaps he should have been speaking with a credit counselor? Spending time doing these things (rather than worrying) could have helped.

Rehashing the past or guessing about the future will not help an illness either, although I've learned that it is helpful to examine the past in order to learn from it. Having had four brain hemorrhages, I have learned that all four came immediately after I engaged in strenuous or stressful activity—causing my blood pressure to go sky high. Thus, I now avoid strenuous and stressful situations.

I also learned that taking aspirin and other blood thinning medications was not good for a person with my condition. Thin blood is not good when you bleed because it causes the bleeding to be more severe, taking longer to clot. So I avoid blood thinning foods, medications, vitamins, and minerals. But, I don't beat myself up for having done these things in the past.

Looking to the past also helped keep things in perspective during my recoveries. Occasionally I would become discouraged with the pace of my recovery. Neurological functions came back slowly, and it was hard for me to see the improvements I had made. I especially became concerned about my physical appearance (vanity—shame on me!). My face was still droopy, my eye was still bloodshot and hurting, and my vision was still blurred. My wife had taken a photograph of me just six weeks after surgery. Boy, did I look ugly! I kept that photograph on my home office desk, and when I became discouraged about the way I looked, all I had to do was look at the photograph. I was quickly reminded of how much progress I had actually made and was given renewed hope that more progress was yet to come.

So a look back at the past can be useful—as a learning experience or reinforcement of just how far you've come in your recovery. But to stay in the present moment, you must also avoid obsessing about the future. It did me no good to try to anticipate the future. I'm not a fortuneteller. I don't have ESP. So worrying about what might or might not happen was counterproductive.

So have I always been successful in staying in the present moment? Unfortunately the answer is no. But I have gotten much better at it over time. Today, when I find myself obsessing about something that might happen tomorrow, next week, or even next year, I have a two-pronged approach for bringing myself back to the present moment.

1. I examine the issue and ask myself how likely (or most usually unlikely) it is to happen. For instance, after my first hemorrhage I lost my job. I was in the early stages of recovery—not knowing when or if I would get better—and suddenly had unemployment to worry about. My mind immediately jumped to the future. What if I couldn't get another job? After

all, who would hire a brain-damaged person like me. What if I couldn't support my family? Who would pay for my sons' college education? What if we lost our home because I was unemployed?

Then I took a step backward and looked at the facts.

- Fact one: I had worked for a great company with a generous disability program. My family would be taken care of for at least a year. A year should be plenty of time to get back on my feet.

- Fact two: My doctor was telling me I would make a full recovery. Why should I doubt my doctor?

- Fact three: It is unlawful *not* to hire someone due to health problems, unless they are physically unable to perform the job. I had a desk job and worked with my brain. My cognitive skills were still strong, so this shouldn't be an issue.

- Fact four: I was a highly sought after person in the job market. Recruiters and executive search firms called me all the time asking if I was ready to change jobs. I hadn't been, but I had kept their names and numbers; I was sure they would still be interested.

My conclusion was that it was unlikely that I would be jobless, homeless, and in financial need. In fact, my conclusion was just the opposite. I concluded that that I would probably be just fine. And I was.

2. If, after going through step one, I am still fretting about an issue, I develop a "plan" and then set it aside. This is a tactic I recently learned from a good

friend. And it works. Make a plan for something that might happen, and then consider the matter dealt with.

For instance, I worried a lot about whether my latest surgery would be successful. Everyone told me there was a chance that I would suffer additional nerve damage during the procedure and come out even worse off. Two neurosurgeons had turned me down, saying the surgery was just too risky. I was frustrated that my surgery date wasn't scheduled sooner—I waited a total of six weeks. So I developed a plan.

- I could always say no to surgery, right up to the last moment, should I still feel uncertain about it.

- In the meantime, I would use the time get physically stronger so that my recovery would be easier. I knew that surgery would weaken my body further; the stronger I was physically going into surgery, the better off I would be after surgery.

- I would do additional research on my condition, my doctors, and the hospital facility to reinforce the fact that I was getting the best care possible.

- I would talk to friends and co-workers about my situation and get their views.

- I would pray for God's guidance and help.

- I would ask others to pray for my successful surgery.

At this point I knew I was doing all that I could. I was able to set aside my surgery worries in favor of executing the six-step plan above.

The present moment is a gift—that's why we call it a *present*. There are times when it is appropriate to remember the past so as to learn from it, or to remember good things with joy, but in fact the past is gone. There are times when we need to think about the future, to do planning. But the future and fantasy are not actually here. The only moment that is real is the present moment.

BE KIND—
ESPECIALLY TO
YOUR CAREGIVERS

"The best portion of a good man's life. His little nameless, unremembered acts of kindness and love."

William Wordsworth
English poet (1770–1850)

My wife was my primary caregiver throughout my illnesses. She helped me dress when I couldn't do it myself. She helped me walk when I needed someone to lean on—literally. She cooked me salmon, broccoli, and spinach, and she fixed me banana milkshakes when my healing body craved these special foods. She chauffeured me around when I couldn't drive, taking me to emergency rooms and doctors' offices. She stayed with me right up to surgery, and then visited me daily in the hospital. She was my cheerleader when my spirits dropped. I couldn't have gone through my many illnesses without her.

Doctors get a lot of well-deserved credit for the healing

they provide, and I am grateful for the exceptional doctors that I hired to fix my body. But I am also grateful for my nurses, receptionists, therapists, pharmacists, and the parking lot attendant, all of whom provided tremendous care to me as I recovered.

Yes, the parking lot attendant. After my last hemorrhage and bleed, I got to know the parking lot attendant at the hospital on a first name basis. We were there at least three times a week for months on end. He always took great care of our vehicle. And he always greeted us by name, with a smile and with kind words, no matter how busy he was.

Doctors are well-compensated for their work, but in my humble opinion, nurses, nurses' aids, pharmacists, receptionists, therapists, and all the rest of the key caregivers are vastly underpaid. I believe it takes a very special person to work in the healthcare industry, especially if they aren't well compensated.

My sister-in-law is a nurse. She is undoubtedly one of the best nurses in the world. She, like many nurses, knows as much about medicine as some doctors. It was nice to be able to pick up the phone and call her when something didn't seem quite right. She gave me a lot of great advice.

I recently told her how grateful I was that she was who she is: 1) a caring nurse, 2) the mother of six children, 3) a loving sister-in-law, and 4) a rock for a lot of people. She told me thanks. She also told me that she understands the fear and panic that most people feel when dealing with sickness, and that sometimes all she needs to do is hold their hand and talk to them. God bless her and all the other nurses in this world who are willing to just hold a patient's hand!

During the time I was hospitalized for my last surgery, I

was worn out and ready to go to bed for the night by 7:00 p.m. Hospital policy was that nighttime medications were distributed at 9:00 p.m.

I was lucky enough to have several nurses who delivered my nighttime medications at 7:00 p.m. every night. These ladies and gentlemen did this for me even though shift change occurred at 7:00 p.m.—a very busy time for them. This way I didn't have to be awakened at 9:00 p.m. just to take a few pills. I was able to sleep until midnight when another nurse checked my vital signs and neurological functions.

Yes, many health professionals are grossly underpaid. But as a patient, I could make up for some of this through my actions and words. By being kind. By not complaining or whining. I made it a point to know and remember their names, their interests, their working hours, and their days off. I always called them by name. And I was never grumpy or unhappy with them, even when they woke me up at 2:00 a.m. for medications, neurological checks, or to take my vitals. Yes, even at 2:00 a.m., still half asleep, I greeted them with cheerfulness and called them by name.

And I always said thank you. When they gave me a shot, I said thank you, and I complemented them by saying, "I hardly felt that. You did a great job!" The same goes for the times when they changed my IV, brought me medications, checked my blood pressure, changed my bed linens, and all the other things these wonderful people did for me. I was as kind to my caregivers as I was to my family and friends. I just appreciated everything they did for me.

And I never complained about anything. Not even hospital food. Do you know that the overall quality and taste of hospital food is the thing patients complain about most often? But, think about it. First, the food must be prepared for a small army of people. It needs to be bland—not much seasoning, salt, pepper, sugar, etc.—to accommodate the dietary restrictions of some patients. We should expect that hospital food will not taste as good as what we eat in a restaurant or at home.

Although hospital food may be bland, mass produced, and not very exciting, at least it is nutritious. In any case, complaining to a nurse or nurse's aid about the food in the hospital is like telling your dentist you're not happy about your insurance coverage. He or she hears this complaint constantly but there is not a thing they can do to change it.

Another thing I tried to do was to become as self-reliant as possible as soon as possible. In addition to being underpaid, caregivers are over worked (again my opinion). These people work twelve-hour shifts and most often have too many patients to attend to.

Immediately after a brain hemorrhage or brain surgery, I was bed ridden and needed help with just about everything. But as soon as I was able and as soon as the doctor cleared it, I began to do things for myself, taking some of the work of caring for me off my caregivers and, at the same time, freeing their time to work with others who needed help more than I did.

In the hospital it was things such as getting out of bed to use the bathroom on my own, rather than using an in-bed urinal. Getting my own drinking water, showering myself, and dressing myself. I did everything I could do for myself as soon as I was able.

My wife is so good to me. She spent hours in the hospital visiting me. She brought me stuff from home, including food. After I was home, she helped me dress, she cooked anything I wanted, she brought my food and drinks to my chair or bed. She set her alarm for 2:00 a.m. and got up to give me medications. She timed her errands so that she was only gone while I was napping. She drove me to doctor and therapy appointments. She even prepared our 2005 federal tax return (she had never prepared a tax return in her life). Her entire life was devoted to caring for me.

Again my objective, to get back to normal as quickly as possible, coincided with my objective of caring for myself as quickly as possible. As soon as I was able to make my own coffee, sandwiches, and soup I did so. As soon as I was able to apply my own medications, I did. As soon as I was able to drive myself to the doctor's office, I was cruising.

In summary:

1. Doctors get a lot of well-deserved credit for helping the sick, but they are also well compensated.

2. Other caregivers (nurses, nurses' aids, receptionists, pharmacists, and yes, even parking lot attendants) are underpaid, overworked, and don't get nearly enough credit for helping the sick.

3. As patients we can help. We can treat our caregivers with kindness, respect, and dignity. We can turn off the whining button. We can say thank you every time they do something for us. And, we can become as self-reliant as we can be as quickly as possible, easing their burden while at the same time freeing them up to take care of other patients who need them more than we do.

THE NEW NORMAL

I will repeat. My goal immediately after each of my six illnesses was to recover fully—to get back to normal as soon as possible. It typically took me a full year to recover, albeit with steady and significant progress along the way.

But in the end, it was always a different normal. The trauma of enduring a serious illness took a toll on me. Headaches were an everyday occurrence for months. And then there was my physical body, which although repaired, was not the same.

My illness was quite obvious, especially in the early days. Once I was sitting in the airport waiting area, about to board an airplane a few months after my latest surgery, when the gate attendant approached me and asked if I needed assistance with early boarding. I mean, he was getting ready to line me up with the mothers with small children, the elderly, and the infirmed. His intentions were good.

Similarly, I visited my mother shortly after she moved into an assisted living facility about two months after my last surgery. A nurse entered the room, saw me sitting at the end of my mother's hospital bed, and asked how *I* was feeling that day. Then she saw my mother lying in bed and suddenly realized my mother was the patient—not me.

It was incidents such as these that made me realize how brain-damaged I must look.

I am not complaining. I am not whining. I'm just stating the facts. This was my *new normal.*

I began writing this chapter just six months after my surgery. At that time there were still several things wrong with me. Today it has been ten months since my surgery. I have made great progress over these past four months, and today my new normal is practically my old normal. Given the number of bleeds, the severity of the bleeds, the location of the bleeds, and the initial severity of the nerve damage, I am a very blessed man. I am happy and grateful to have what I have.

I know others with the same illness that are in wheelchairs, are bed bound, and who require round the clock care. Me? I can walk. I can care for myself. I can drive. I can play golf. I can inspire others. I can help those in need. I can do most everything I want to do. And I have the rest of my life to continue to improve. There is just no reason to be bitter.

I accept my few weaknesses and have adjusted my life to the new normal. For instance, I never go anywhere without my reading glasses. Before my last episode, I needed reading glasses only on rare occasions. Now, with my impaired vision, I can't read a thing without my glasses. Even then it is difficult. So I have purchased a pair of accordion-style fold-up glasses that fit in a very tiny holder, and I carry these glasses in my pocket everywhere I go.

I drive, but not for long distances. The strain on my eye is just too painful. I have purchased a hearing aid to help restore my hearing. I don't smile anymore because I can't—the muscles on the left side of my mouth are paralyzed. I am investigating plastic surgery to lift my slightly drooping left eye and mouth—not for the sake of vanity, but to be more functional. You see, my slightly droopy eye still causes me some strain and pain, and my sagging mouth still causes me to drool a slight bit when drinking and eating.

I play golf. Because of my impaired vision, I can't always see the golf ball after I hit it. One of my golfing buddies helps me watch where my ball goes. He has been my second pair of eyes for months!

I could go on and on, but I won't. I prefer not to dwell on the negatives.

Christopher Reeve, in his book *Still Me*, talks about how he adjusted his life after a tragic equestrian accident transformed him from a fully functioning, healthy movie star (*Superman*) to a quadriplegic. He turned his talents to inspirational speaking (I was lucky enough to hear one such speech) and directing films. Together with his wife, he set up an organization that, even after both their demise, successfully raises money for spinal injury research. He made the maximum use of the body, mind, and spirit he had. He made the optimum use of his new normal.

I've adjusted my life to account for the few issues that

have not yet healed. I am looking forward, not backward. I am plunging ahead, living as active a life as I am able. And I still hold out hope for a full recovery. My new normal is different—not better and not worse—just different.

CONCLUSION

"The truth that many people never understand, until it is too late, is that the more you try to avoid suffering the more you suffer because smaller and more insignificant things begin to torture you in proportion to your fear of being hurt."

Thomas Merton
US. Religious author, clergyman, & Trapist monk
(1915–1968)

This was a hard book for me to write. It was much more difficult to write than my first book, *They Made you the Boss, Now What?*.

I began writing just two months after my last surgery when I was still in the early stages of recovery. The first few chapters took a lot of time, because I was only strong enough to sit at the computer and type for short periods of time. Writing about how I have recovered from six serious brain episodes also dredged up unpleasant memories. I completed writing the initial manuscript ten months after my last brain surgery.

As I reflect on what I have been through, I realize that

I hate this genetic illness, which makes me prone to hemorrhages in my brain that sometimes dictate brain surgeries. I hate the disruption it has caused in my life—literally placing things on hold for months at a time. I hate the pain, suffering, and anguish it has caused my family and me. I hate that my son and my mother suffer from the same affliction. I pray that my grandchildren will not inherit my bad genes.

I feel as though no human being should have to go through what I've been through. And the thing I pray for the most is that I will never have to go through it again. I have several more vascular malformations in my brain, brainstem, and spine. I pray every day that God will watch over me and not allow another one to bleed.

There. I got that off my chest. I feel much better.

The bottom line is that I have survived four brain hemorrhages and two brain surgeries in the past sixteen years.

I am currently retired and on disability, not just because of the residual nerve damage from my hemorrhages, but because—given the number of malformed veins remaining in my brain, brainstem, and spine and my history of bleeding—the doctor recommended that I eliminate the stress of work from my life.

I realize that some people don't recover from serious illness. I realize that some people even die. I realize that some people get worse, not better. But I also realize that an *army* of people out there do survive, recover, and get better. That is what I want to dwell on—the fact that most people survive to thrive. And, praise the Lord, I am one of them! And with continued advancements in modern medicine, even more will get a second, a third, or as in my case, a sixth chance.

A serious illness is a scary thing. Whether it is a brain hemorrhage, cancer, heart disease, AIDS, or whatever else the illness might be. It is natural and understandable to be frightened. It is acceptable to be angry and to look for the "cause."

What I have learned most by going through this six times is that I was better off if I didn't stay frightened, angry, and accusatory. My last recovery from the worst neurological damage I suffered was the smoothest, because I stayed positive and didn't lose faith that my health would be normal again.

There are ten main messages I wanted to convey in this book. Here they are in my favorite Top Ten list style:

Top Ten Ways I Survived a Catastrophic Illness (Six Times)

1. By keeping my spiritual and emotional health strong—my physical health followed in time.

2. By *knowing* that I *would* recover.

3. By realizing that my physical sufferings were only temporary.

4. By making recovery my full-time job. It was hard work—perhaps the hardest thing I've ever done—but the results are worth it.

5. By keeping my sense of humor, and making sure I got some regular laugh therapy.

6. By proactively making sure that I got the very best doctors, facilities, and treatments available. After all, I deserved it.

7. By becoming a nuisance when the medical system wasn't moving at the pace I thought it should.

8. By praying a lot—both talking to and listening to God.

9. By staying positive.

10. By listening to my body—and seeking immediate medical attention at the first sign of problems.

AFTERWORD

It is May 20, 2007—my fifty-ninth birthday. I am a bit amused that many men and women would try to hide their age on their birthday—especially if that age is fifty-nine. I, on the other hand, am proud to have made it this far. For me, every birthday is a cause for great celebration.

I had lunch with a friend today who said, "Les, you look remarkably good. I haven't seen you since October and the improvement is amazing!" Another friend recently told me, "You look normal." (To which I replied that I had never looked normal.) Still another person told me that my recovery was miraculous! I love it when people refer to me as a "walking miracle" or "an inspiration for how someone should cope with a catastrophic illness." Even I am amazed at the enormous progress I have made.

Fortunately, we human beings have the ability to forget things. I have forgotten just how bleak my situation was following my last hemorrhage. I have forgotten how weakened I was from my last surgery. I just don't think about it. Instead, I concentrate on what I still have, and I am eternally grateful that God has given me back things like walking, seeing, hearing, and so many other gifts that I once took for granted.

My once droopy eye is 90% healed, my droopy face is symmetrical once again, my droopy mouth is barely noticeable, and my hearing is "good enough" without a hearing aid and almost perfect with an aid.

More importantly, I can walk, I can talk, I can eat, and I can care for myself. I am no longer easily fatigued. My daily headaches are gone. Am I back to normal? Not quite. But this is my new normal. And I have the rest of my life to continue recovering.

I thank God every day for blessing me with this recovery and with all the other recoveries from previous episodes. With four brain hemorrhages and two brain surgeries under my belt, I am a fully functional human being. I look forward to seeing my sons get married. I look forward to meeting my grandchildren. And I look forward to a long and active retirement with my wife, Sharon.

Nearly everyone knows someone who is dealing with a catastrophic illness—a friend, a co-worker, a family member. I wrote this book to offer sage advice and wisdom on coping with and surviving the pain, grief, fear, and frustration that goes with a catastrophic illness—something I have firsthand experience with.

I hope that you or someone you love can learn from my experiences. I hope it will help you or someone you love get through a difficult time. I pray that it will provide inspiration and hope for someone in a difficult situation.

ENDNOTES

1   Wooten, Patty. 1991. Jest for the Health of It! Creating a Comedy Cart. http://www.jesthealth.com/art04jnj.html. (accessed August 21, 2006).

2   American Cancer Society. ACS: Humor Therapy. http://cancer. org/docroot/ETO_53X_Humor. (accessed August 21, 2006)

3   Bultz, Barry D PhD. and Holland, Jimmie C M.D. Psychosocial Oncology. Emotional distress in patients with cancer: the sixth vital sign. http://www.communityoncology.net/journal/articles/0305311.pdf (accessed on September 23, 2006)

4   Self Knowledge.com. Dictionary Information: Definition of Patience. http://www.selfknowledge.com/69354.htm (accessed October 23, 2006)

5   Fun Trivia.com, Answers to everything. http://www.funtrivia. com/askft/Question67654.html (accessed on October 2, 2006)

6   Wikipedia, the free encyclopedia. Cooties. http://en.wikipedia. org/wiki/Cooties (accessed May 25, 2006)

7   Catholic Online: Prayers. Prayers for the Sick and Prayers for Healing, http://www.catholic.org/clife/prayers/prayer.php?p=74 (accessed May 14, 2006)

8   Ibid.

9   Ibid.

10 Ibid.

11 Ibid.

12 AOL Hometime. Mary's Collection of Catholic Prayers. Catholic Prayers for the Sick. http://members.aol.com/mstringy13/page14.html (accessed May 15, 2006)

13 Cowpi.com. May today there be peace within. http://journal.cowpi.com/2004/10/may_today_there_be_peace_within (accessed May 18, 2006)

14 EWTN Global Catholic Network . Saint Anthony of Padua Novena. Day One. http://www.ewtn.com/devotionals/novena/anthony.htm (accessed May 21, 2006)

15 EWTN Glocal Catholic Netowrk. Father John Corapi, SOLT. End Game, unity, truth, good beauty. Caught in the crossfire. ATTACK/COUNTER-ATTACK. (viewed April 5, 2006)